Choice Knowledge for Students

Words of Wisdom

Barbara D. Culp

Glean knowledge and wisdom from the experiences of someone who has successfully traversed the roads of education. Written for educators and learners in all walks of the educational journey, *Words of Wisdom* provides a collection of guiding principles, practical advice, and encouraging words for both beginners and veterans in the world of education.

Other Titles in This Series

Vintage Knowledge for Principals: Keys to Enrich, Encourage, and Empower School Leaders and Empowering Today's Principals
Essential Knowledge for Teachers: Truths to Energize, Excite, and Engage Today's Teachers
Trusted Knowledge for Parents: Tips to Prepare, Position, and Empower Today's Parents

Choice Knowledge for Students

Words to Empower, Enliven, and Enrich Your Life

Barbara D. Culp

ROWMAN & LITTLEFIELD
Lanham • Boulder • New York • London

Published by Rowman & Littlefield
A wholly owned subsidiary of The Rowman & Littlefield Publishing Group, Inc.
4501 Forbes Boulevard, Suite 200, Lanham, Maryland 20706
www.rowman.com

Unit A, Whitacre Mews, 26-34 Stannary Street, London SE11 4AB

British Library Cataloguing in Publication Information Available

Library of Congress Cataloging-in-Publication Data Available

ISBN 978-1-4758-3505-2 (pbk. : alk. paper)

∞™ The paper used in this publication meets the minimum requirements of American National Standard for Information Sciences—Permanence of Paper for Printed Library Materials, ANSI/NISO Z39.48-1992.

Printed in the United States of America

This book is dedicated to my beloved grandchildren and great-grandchildren. As a lifelong educator who is passionate about teaching and learning, I have always desired to have at least one of you follow in my footsteps. As of this printing, you have all spread your wings in other directions. Oh, well. There is still hope with the great-great-grandchildren!

I offer this Choice Knowledge to make your path in life clearer, richer, and more fulfilling.

Love you all!

"The great thing in this world is not so much where we are, but in what direction we are moving."

—Oliver Wendell Holmes

Contents

Foreword

Congratulations! If you are reading this page, it means that you have taken the most important step toward receiving the awesome wisdom that Dr. Barbara D. Culp has provided for you in this book. Each page contains a golden "wisdom nugget" that will help you on your journey to becoming an exquisite learner and academic superstar!

I have spent many years coaching people in all walks of life. During that time, I have noticed that no matter how educated the person, where they live, or how old they are—everyone has this one thing in common. Every day we all make thousands of decisions about what we will think, feel, and do. Some researchers say we make as many as sixty thousand decisions in a day! From what clothing to put on, what to eat for lunch, or what to say to the people who talk to you—your brain is busy helping you make choices about your life.

As you consider this mind-blowing reality, I'd like you to also think about two other things. First, every choice you make has consequences. For example, if you choose to study for a test, you can make a good grade. If you choose not to study, you probably will not do so well on the test. If you eat too much, you will gain weight. If you get enough sleep at night you will feel rested when you wake up in the morning. If you are nice to people, they will be nice to you (most of the time, anyway).

Second—and this is the good news—you are in charge of your choices! That means you have the power to choose to be excellent, and you can choose to think of yourself as a smart and capable learner.

No one can make you feel small or insult you without your permission! You can choose to respect others and yourself, and you can also choose to be kind. You have the power to choose to work hard or not to work at all. Each moment you choose what you will think, feel, and say. That is tremendous power!

I believe that God has created you with your own unique set of talents. You already have all the necessary tools to be successful. Dr. Culp gives you a roadmap for making choices that will allow you to develop your strengths and be all that God created you to be. The choice knowledge described on every page will help you to shape the decisions you make about yourself and lead you to excellent outcomes in your life.

One of my favorite things about Dr. Culp is that she is always a student because she is always open to learning new things. She is an amazing teacher who is passionate about passing on to others what she learns so they can benefit from it. Because I too am *always a student*, I have learned many things from her over the years. I am grateful for the way she generously shares herself with those who are willing to receive and who are ready to grow. I know that you too will grow in some amazing ways when you are thoughtful and take care to embrace the words of wisdom on these pages that are the result of Dr. Culp's rich experiences as a master educator.

Enjoy reading and have a great journey!

Faye Hargrove, PhD
Author, *Better Choices*
www.betterchoices.guru

Preface

You have probably been told many times that the choices you make now will follow you for the rest of your life. I can tell you that it's absolutely true—and that it's a wonderful, powerful thing!

If you're eight years old or eighteen years old, today marks the starting line for the rest of your life. But you're not about to take off on a race that might find you at the end of the pack and therefore the loser. Instead, the race is all about feeling the wind under your wings! The more you follow your passions, the faster you will run. The faster you run, the farther you will go!

It all starts right here with the book you hold in your hands. In these pages, you will be reminded that you are a valuable human being. The contributions you will make to this world along with the contributions you have already made will shine! Whenever you reach farther or push that extra little bit, the greatness within you becomes even brighter.

Your job is to take every opportunity to learn, to grow, and to become the person you were meant to be in this world. And you won't walk this road alone. The friends you hold so dear to your heart will be right there with you. The teachers and parents who care so much about you will give you a boost whenever you need a little help. The eyes of the entire world are on you, our youth. They all want you to succeed!

The wisdom in this book is my gift to you. Little keepsakes are wrapped into every word. Each gift weighs nothing but its value can't be measured. Accept those gifts that will help you and feel free to set the rest aside. Live always as if your destiny is within reach and you will succeed!

Acknowledgments

I acknowledge that being a student today is not easy. I also acknowledge that schoolwork can be hard and that in some instances, teachers might not teach in ways that make learning easy or fun. Don't let that keep you from getting the education you so richly deserve. Take it upon yourself to seek out the right people and the best strategies so you can get the most from every subject. You are a diamond in the rough. You are more valuable than you know! All you need is the right people to breathe over you and gently polish you with love until you sparkle and shine!

Seek out the wisdom of a supportive community of believers. Appreciate what each person can offer you. Their experiences in life, different careers, and travel can save you time and steer you away from the potholes. Their wisdom can propel you to the front of your class!

Don't ever think that because you live in the projects, a trailer park, or your parents don't hold the best jobs you cannot achieve greatness. Excellence springs from innate beliefs. It is an inborn trait that magnetically draws you to the one career where you will shine and make a difference. We all have it; we just have to be exposed to the right experience to find our unique place in this world.

Embrace the *Choice Knowledge* in this book and I promise that you will emerge as an academic leader ahead of your peers who have not read this book.

Introduction

Too often you've been told to wait until you're older. You've been told you won't understand. You're too young, you don't know what you're doing, or you can't. I'm here to tell you that you can!

You are America's greatest asset. You are building the future of a society where people want to live. You are creating a place where everyone can live well. A lot of that depends on the education you receive today. Education isn't just about tests and grades and homework. Your heart and your soul are also growing!

This book provides the wisdom you need as you grow and change. As you step out into the world armed with this wisdom, you'll realize that only you can define beauty—and the most beautiful people are kind and honest. The haters and the fakers and the "cool" kids don't have any power over you because you are a powerful person in your own right!

How do I know? Because I worked at different schools for forty years. Half of that time I spent teaching. The other half I spent as a principal of a school very much like yours. I worked with kids who had learning disabilities and those who were at the top of their grades. Some of the students transferred in at the middle of the year and fit right in. Others came in on the first day and felt totally lost! I taught black kids and white kids, rich ones and poor ones. I helped some students catch up with their schooling and waved others off to college.

Every one of those young people had goals and dreams. Every one of them also needed a little guidance or extra help. They all had strengths—some that lay hidden and others that blazed brightly! Every one of those kids got 100 percent of my attention. Because I want to keep helping students like them and like you, I decided to write this book.

Choice Knowledge for Students is divided into three categories. In the first one, Choice Knowledge for Your Power, you'll find guidance on building and nurturing your inner strength. The second section, Choice Knowledge for Your Balance, shows you how to build a stable foundation so you can handle school, work, family, friends, and all the other things you juggle! The third section is Choice Knowledge for Your Life. There you'll find great ways to supercharge your journey day by day, year after year.

Each section has individual entries that offer different types of wisdom. Each piece of wisdom is defined in a very short sentence. The next paragraph lays out the benefits of that wisdom. An example of how that wisdom applies to school is offered in the third paragraph. The last paragraph lists specific and easy ways you can use the wisdom in your life!

Check it out a little at a time or read the entire book in about an hour. Keep *Choice Knowledge for Students* handy so you can look up the easy tips whenever you want to try something new. Reread the book every summer right before you return to school or right after you start the midyear break. As you grow, you'll find new ways to use the wisdom. You'll grow even faster and take charge of your life. And that's a real reason to say, "Wow!"

Part I

Choice Knowledge for Your Power

DON'T WAIT

Don't wait for your life to begin. You're living it now!

When you *don't wait*, you grab each opportunity as it arrives. You recognize that your future dreams depend on the actions you take today. Every step, even small or boring ones, will pay off when you achieve the goals you've set!

Don't wait for the perfect teacher, your favorite subject, or the support of your friends to really focus on school. Don't wait until you turn a certain age to do something just because everyone else thinks you're too young. Don't wait for everyone else to think something is cool if it's really what you want!

When you *don't wait,* you follow your inner compass. You locate the place on the map where you really want to go, and you chart the course that takes you there. When you strike out early, you arrive ahead of your peers. Every time you achieve another goal, you'll discover new friends waiting to greet you. You'll learn that you are able to do much more than you thought possible. You'll know yourself better and believe in yourself!

JUST ASK

Just ask for help, and you'll help yourself!

Just ask for help whenever you need it. Asking for help from teachers puts all their experience and knowledge in your hands. Asking your friends for help gives you a new perspective. When you ask for help from other adults, you reach outside of the school and find all kinds of support!

Just asking proves that you're growing. Seeking assistance is part of the process of getting older. When you question how things could be done better, you're opening up to new ideas. You'll learn ways to do things you didn't know before. You'll become a better person and a better student at the same time!

Just ask is a very simple way to think about something that can feel very hard. Some students think that asking for help means they're not as smart as the other students. Nothing could be further from the truth! Asking proves that you're curious. It shows that you want to become better than you already are. You're growing and changing every day of your life. So much is ahead of you, and now is the time to really reach!

THINK FOR YOURSELF

Think for yourself no matter what your friends and peers do.

Think for yourself because you are the only person who can take really good care of you. No matter how much the adults in your life want to keep you safe, only you are around all the time. When you think for yourself, you'll always find the safest and best way through any challenge.

Thinking for yourself is really important at school. The other students are older and younger than you. They come from different backgrounds and have lived different lives. They don't always share your values, and they don't all care about themselves. When you think for yourself, you make judgments that are best for you!

Think for yourself whenever things get tough or scary. Your friends might invite you to try drugs "just for fun." The cool kids might pull dangerous stunts. Some adults might ask you to do things that aren't right or that make you uncomfortable. Thinking for yourself can be difficult. If you're in doubt, just walk away! The world will not fall apart just because you take time to think about whether you want to do something.

RESCUE YOURSELF

Rescue yourself by taking charge of your body, your mind, and your spirit.

The sooner you learn how to *rescue yourself,* the more powerful you will become. By taking charge of yourself in the moment, you peel away all the passive, do-nothing weight that drags you down. You cut away all the people and things that hurt you. You make room for happy friends and positive events!

Almost every student has to *rescue themselves* at some point when they attend school. No one is a genius in all subjects, so everyone needs help at some point. Teachers, tutors, fellow students, and the adults in your life might be able to help you figure things out. And if they can't help, they probably know someone who can! Remember that teachers ask each other for help all the time. They're rescuing themselves by reaching out. You can too!

Rescue yourself by paying attention to the kind of people you hang out with. So many of the things students need help with involve other people: peers who pressure them to do things they don't want to do, bullies who are just plain mean, and friends who want someone to share the blame with when they're caught doing something wrong. Step back from those kinds of people and you'll rescue yourself before trouble starts!

SPEAK UP

Speak up to let your voice be heard.

Speak up to gain power in your world. Speaking effectively ensures that people listen to you—and that they understand what you're saying! When you are heard, you are able to ask for what you need. You're able to explain your thoughts and ideas, and you can present your feelings in a way that captures support.

Speaking up is an important tool. At the ground level, you need to speak up to connect with the kinds of people who will become loyal friends. In class, you need to be able to present your ideas and explain your way of doing things so you can learn new ideas and methods. Outside the classroom, you'll encounter people from every background. When you know how to speak up, you're better able to communicate with all of them!

Speak up by knowing, first and foremost, that you have something to say. Your input is important to your peers and the adults around you. Then think about what you have to share. If you've found a solution no one else has considered, you'll have to explain the new idea so that everyone can understand. Then consider who you're talking to. If you're helping a friend who really struggles with a math problem, you might have to help them learn a more basic math skill first. Once you know these three things, speaking up is much easier!

FIGHT SMART

Fight smart by fighting with your mind, not with your fists.

Fighting smart gives you a power that's better than physical strength. When you use your intelligence to tackle challenges, you find creative solutions. You cut scary problems down to size and spend less time worrying. Best of all, fighting smart keeps you safe!

Fight smart when faced with bullies. First, get away from them by taking the fastest escape route! Then talk to someone about the problem. If the bully is insulting or gets others to gang up on you, your mind is your best defense. Remember who you are. Keep your mind focused on getting away and then getting help!

Fight smart by looking for an opportunity within a problem. A low grade can be your chance to ask for more help with a particular subject, or you could set up a study group. When the rules prevent you from doing something you want to do, search for an allowed activity you might enjoy just as much. Even when you can't find the opportunity, know that when you solve the problem, you're learning how to think in new ways. That alone is an opportunity to grow!

TAKE TURNS

Take turns to build confidence in your friends and fellow students.

Taking turns is a skill that always reaps rewards. When you take turns, you step back long enough to really pay attention to how someone else does something. You learn new ways of doing things. You also discover that you can help others do things better! And your friends know you care enough to let others have the spotlight.

Taking turns keeps your school running smoothly. Raising your hand in class, standing in line at the cafeteria, and making appointments are all ways people take turns. Taking turns keeps things fair, too. You only have to watch one person cut in line to feel how unfair that is!

Take turns in unique ways. When you are given a group assignment, consider whether one of your fellow students is perfect to lead the group. Invite them to set the pace for the work. Among your friends, you're bound to find one who doesn't talk as much as others. Ask them questions to allow them their turn to share! When you pay attention to other people's turns, you prove that you really care.

DEBATE

When you *debate*, you support your ideas with clear, logical thoughts.

Debate is a calm way to settle important issues—and even ones that might seem less important! When you debate, you avoid the anger and frustration an argument can whip up. People will listen more closely, too. You won't win every debate but you will be heard!

Debate is often used to help students learn. Hearing lectures all the time can be boring, so teachers frequently stop and ask for opinions. This is different from calling on students for an answer—in that case, they are asking for facts. When you debate, you offer an opinion that you support with facts! Once you know how to debate in school, you can use the same skills at home and with friends.

Knowing the difference between a *debate* and an argument helps a lot. Arguments happen when two or more people won't listen to each other. Debates take place when both sides listen, ask questions, and try to see things from the other person's view. The process respects both sides. No one pushes the other into accepting something. Instead, one side gets the chance to convince the other!

EARN IT

Earning it lets you enjoy the real benefit of working hard: pride in a job well done.

Earning it boosts your self-confidence. When you put in the effort to learn something new or receive an allowance, you prove that you can do whatever is asked. And because the things you want will change as you grow, you'll take different steps to earn different rewards. No matter whether you want better grades, an allowance, or a place on the sports team, earn it to learn it!

Students have to *earn* practically everything at school! Grades and test scores are earned by studying and homework. Slots on the choir, a role in the play, and a spot on any team are earned by learning a special kind of skill. You even have to earn the trust of your teachers and your friends!

Earn it by putting in a real effort. Lessons that are really tough can be frustrating, so ask for help if you need it. When a lesson is really easy for you, help someone else earn it by pitching in. Your efforts will earn you trust, respect, and maybe even a new friend!

BE RESPONSIBLE

Be responsible for yourself—and only yourself!

Being responsible makes you more independent. It turns your attention to your own needs and goals, and makes you more confident. When you take responsibility for yourself, you prove that you're able to make good choices!

One of the ways to *be responsible* in school is to refuse to be responsible for others. You already know that saying no to dangerous activities keeps you safe. You should also never be responsible for risks your friends or fellow students take. You don't get into a car with a driver who has been drinking because you don't want to get hurt when they crash. For the same reason, don't lend money and never cosign for someone else. Those responsibilities belong to someone else!

Be responsible by knowing your limits. Drinking and using drugs are clearly off limits. Other things are clearly yours to decide: completing assignments on time, being a good friend, and keeping your promises are great ways to be responsible. For the gray areas, it's totally all right to say, "Maybe." Take time to think about things you're not sure you want to take on. Take an hour, a day, a week—whatever you need! If anyone pressures you to answer before you are ready, say, "No, thanks!"

KEEP IT REAL

Keeping it real places honesty and truth at the top of your priority list.

Keeping it real moves you forward in a way you can feel good about. Liars have to lie all the time to keep their original lies a secret, and cheaters always get caught. When you practice honesty and truth, your life is a lot less complicated! You get to be who you are. You never have to hide anything you've done or said.

It's very important to *keep it real* at school. A study performed by Rutgers University found that up to 70 percent of high school students admit to a serious form of cheating on tests! Even texting someone test questions is dishonest. People who cheat don't learn today's lessons, which makes tomorrow's work harder. When you earn an honest grade, you discover what you're naturally good at.

Keep it real in every area of your life. Eat well and exercise so you won't feel pressured to cheat at sports. Complete your assignments on time so you don't fall behind. Be honest with your friends, and if your honest opinion will hurt them, find a nice way to help them become better people. When you make honesty and truth your top priority, you gain the trust of your friends, your fellow students, your teachers, and your parents!

STAND ON YOUR OWN

Stand on your own to take control of your life.

Standing on your own builds your confidence and self-worth. You'll grow more independent, and you'll be able to solve problems without anyone's help. You'll also feel confident enough to ask for help when you need it!

One of the primary goals of every school is to teach students to *stand on their own.* Homework might sometimes feel like busy work but really it's about trusting you to take control! Homework assignments are given out with every expectation that they will be turned in on time. That means you and only you control whether it actually gets done! Every study hall and hour spent in the library is another chance for you to practice independence at school.

Stand on your own by knowing how to stay safe in any situation. Learn how to take care of yourself by cooking meals and washing your own clothes. Ask for an allowance so you can buy clothes, school supplies, and anything you need for extracurricular activities. Have your parents help you set up a savings account so you can put money away for special purchases or holiday and birthday gifts. The more you stand on your own, the stronger you become!

THINK IT THROUGH

When you *think it through,* you take all the time you need to consider all sides of a situation.

Thinking it through keeps your mind open and creative. By considering a problem from every angle, you'll realize that it's probably not that big a deal after all! You'll be able to see all the options you have, which lets you pick the best one. You'll meet challenges head on and build your inner strength!

Think it through to perform your best at school. Juggling a lot of assignments and demands can be pretty tough. It's tempting to just give up and stop trying. But that doesn't make the work stop. It just leaves you behind while your friends move ahead! Luckily, schools have lots of resources to help you think things through. Your teachers, a guidance counselor, and even your student government can point out different ways to tackle problems. Thinking it through on your own and with others will solve the problem every time!

Think it through by considering the issue itself. Why did it show up? Could changing one of the reasons it popped up eliminate the problem? If not, consider what you can do about it. When you find more than one way to resolve an issue, you can pick the one that gives you the best results. If you can't find a solution, see if someone else can. By thinking through the issue yourself first, you'll be able to find the right person who can help!

WEIGH YOUR WORDS

Weigh your words because once you've spoken, you can't take them back!

Weighing your words means you never have to regret what you say. You'll only say things that are warm and supportive. Your friends will know that you care about them. You'll make—and keep—friends who will be there for you.

At school, *weigh your words* carefully. Every day you're in class with people who have really different lives than you! Other students and teachers might not know enough about you to understand what you're trying to say. Explain whatever they need to know about you or the situation to make sure that your words say what you really mean!

Always *weigh your words* when talking to other people. If something might come across as hurtful, ask yourself whether it really needs to be said! If you truly do need to speak, think carefully about how you're going to lay out your point. Say what you mean in the nicest possible way. Recognize that saying things face to face is often a lot easier to hear than receiving a text or e-mail. They can't see your concern or hear your tone in writing! Follow up by telling your friend you love them and support them.

KNOW YOUR LIMITS

Know your limits so you stay healthy mentally and physically.

Know your limits and you'll end up happier! First, figuring out what your limits are will help you grow as a person. Once you know what your limits are, you'll achieve more by staying inside those limits. The successes you'll reach will make you confident, and you'll stay healthy while reaching a lot of goals!

It's a lot easier to *know your limits* in school than anywhere else. After all, every test you take and every grade you receive measures how well you're doing. When you get a B on an assignment, you can decide whether that's good enough or whether you want to push for an A the next time. A very low grade tells you that you're working at some kind of limit. In those cases, ask for help moving past your limit!

Know your limits by talking to people you trust. Your best friend might help you figure out why you can't seem to make new friends in a group you've just joined. Teachers and coaches can help you become a leader. They can also help you figure out which activity is the best considering your particular set of skills. And ask yourself! No one knows you better than you do. You probably already know some of your limits. You just have to be honest with yourself!

POSITIVE POWER

Positive power lets you draw from an unlimited source of energy.

Positive power supercharges your days! When you focus on the positive, you are able to accept the way things are. Even better, you can take steps to make improvements. When you charge yourself with positive power, you transfer that power to other people! You feel excited about your life, and any obstacles you face become far less challenging.

Positive power is a great benefit for your school. Positive school environments have less bullying, higher test scores, and students who are happier and more confident. Positive schools even have happier teachers—and that makes everyone more relaxed in the classroom. Best of all, it makes school a place students want to go!

Ramp up your *positive power* by trying new things. Check out groups you've been curious about but haven't had time to research. Try new foods, listen to different types of music, learn a new sport, or eat in a new restaurant. Read whatever book looks like it might be interesting, watch a weird movie, pick an old TV program to stream, and walk a different route to school or the bus stop. The more things you try, the more excitement and fun you'll bring into your life. And that will pump up your positivity!

TEACH YOURSELF

Teach yourself because life is a university!

Teaching yourself opens you up to new possibilities. The world is full of new thoughts and great ideas. Every day of your life is a day when you can learn and grow and expand. Your lessons began long before you started school, and they will continue long after you graduate!

Teaching yourself can help you a lot at school. Every time you finish your homework, you're teaching yourself the assigned lesson. When you read books over the summer, you're teaching yourself about the world and the people in it—and that will help during the academic year. Even playing sports or dance classes can help at school because you're teaching yourself how to listen to an instructor!

Practicing is a form of learning, so every time you practice something, you're *teaching yourself.* When you play sports, you're practicing your skills at the game and teaching yourself. Painting picture after picture is practice, so you're teaching yourself to paint! You can also teach yourself how to think and act in a mature way. Teach yourself and you'll learn faster than ever!

OFFER THANKS

Offer thanks to anyone (or anything) that has helped you.

Offering thanks keeps you focused on the positive things in your life. These two little words, "Thank you," hold an amazing power! Offering thanks shows people that you appreciate everything they do and that you respect who they are. Simple gestures mean so much. Offering thanks might be the simplest and most meaningful of all!

Offering thanks fits right into the school environment. When you think about what happens every day on campus, you realize that hundreds of people have come together to make things work smoothly. Thanking your teacher is an obvious start. You can also thank the police officers who keep the halls safe, the janitors who clean up the buildings, and the crew that cuts the lawns. Coaches, principals, parent volunteers, and a whole bunch of others would love to hear "Thank you!"

Offer thanks to anyone in your life who deserves a little boost. Thank your parents for helping you in all the many, many ways they show they care! Thank your pet for being a great buddy with a good scratch behind the ears. Thank your neighbor for growing all those pretty flowers in their front yard where everyone can enjoy them. And always offer yourself thanks for all the things you do for yourself!

CRY TIME

Cry time happens in those moments when a few tears are good for you—no matter your gender or age!

Cry time is important because tears are a healthy way to deal with emotions. Crying can cut the amount of worry you feel, help you relax, and reduce your stress! After crying, you can see things better because you're calmer. The relief you'll feel will help you tackle whatever caused the tears in the first place!

The people at school know all about *cry time.* Tears are a natural part of life. Since students are learning so much so quickly, it's natural that crying is just going to happen. A student who cries isn't weak or weird. That person is just feeling a whole lot of strong emotions! You might feel more comfortable with a little privacy if you cry at school. Even if you can't find a quiet spot, go ahead and cry. You have nothing to be ashamed of!

It takes a strong, self-aware person to allow for *cry time!* Tears are our body's natural healers. They literally wash out the chemicals our body creates during stressful times. On top of that, tears clean our hearts of sadness and anger. After crying, our breathing and our heart rate slow down. That makes us calmer, and a calm mind can look at things in a new way. Allow yourself time for tears and you'll end up much happier!

TURN ENVY AROUND

Turn envy around to make it work for you!

When you *turn envy around,* you use a powerful feeling to spur your growth. Feeling jealous about someone else's success means that you want to achieve the same thing! Recognize that this goal could be yours, and you'll grow into a bigger, better person.

Turn envy around in the classroom. That pang you feel when the highest grade isn't on your paper means that you can do better. Think about whether you are really putting in your best effort. Ask whether there are books or other resources that will help you learn the subject faster. If you're already doing everything you know to do, ask for a tutor!

Turn envy around by realizing that jealousy is a message from your inner self. Envy tells you that you have a passion for something specific—so follow that passion! Be positive about the new steps you're taking to achieve that goal. Congratulate the person who has already gained that success. You can even ask how they got where they are! When you turn envy around, you harness the power of your own passion to succeed.

THE RIGHT OPPORTUNITY

The right opportunity is the one that takes you closer to success.

Seizing *the right opportunity* gives you power over your own happiness. Not every opportunity is right for you, so being able to cut out the wrong ones keeps you focused. Every time you choose the right opportunity, you choose to control your present and your future!

Plenty of *right opportunities* wait for you at school. Every subject is an opportunity to learn about new things. Every classroom offers dozens of opportunities to connect with new friends. Every lunch break is the opportunity to select healthy food that will fuel your body and your mind. Even the time you spend walking to class is an opportunity to think about your choices!

Find *the right opportunities* by recognizing that you don't have to seize every opportunity! When a friend turns mean and says terrible things, you don't have to be mean back. You don't have to attend every party or social event your friends do, and you certainly don't have to follow along when they do something you know is wrong. Select the right opportunities that will lead to your growth, your independence, and your courage!

STRETCH IT

Stretching it achieves goals that must be accomplished with one big effort.

Stretch it to create something bigger than yourself. When you reach stretch goals, you use all your skills to make a huge difference in your life. And by tackling something that is very difficult, you gain pride and a sense of accomplishment!

Stretch it at school. You might decide to lift your grade point average across all your classes as an academic stretch goal. If you want to focus on personal growth, you might decide to become more patient with others during the school year. These kinds of goals require you to put in a focused effort. You'll also have to use many of your skills to achieve them! Stretch goals are challenging—and because of that, they are worth the effort!

When you *stretch it,* use a single image to inspire you. Think of a person you admire for having met the same goal. What values do you think they hold? Match up those values to your own. Think about how you try to live up to those values. Then decide which values will help you meet your stretch goal. If the values you need aren't high on your list, how can you practice that value so it becomes a stronger force in your life? When you stay focused on those values, your motivation will soar and you'll stretch toward that goal!

PACK YOUR TOOLBOX

Pack your toolbox with the attitudes and habits you need to build your life.

When you *pack your toolbox* with the right things, you set yourself up for success on all kinds of levels. Having the right tools allows you to take action the moment you see the need. You feel great about yourself and the life you're leading. You take fewer risks that can lead you into danger. Your mind is healthy, and that keeps you happy!

Pack your toolbox for school with loads of self-esteem. If your test score isn't as high as you'd like, remember that you'll have a chance to do better with the next test. Remember that bullies and mean kids are very unhappy. Put up a wall they can't climb by staying happy with yourself. Allow yourself to have bad days now and then. Tomorrow will always arrive, and you will bounce back!

Pack your toolbox with at least three important tools. Use the magnifying glass of your intelligence to study each new situation. When you think through how things are going, you can decide whether to stay in that situation or change things. Always have the blanket of confidence available to wrap yourself in warmth. And use the light of love to chase away the shadows, find your path, and guide others. What other tools will you pack in your toolbox?

REAL ROLE-PLAYING

Real role-playing helps you develop important skills without taking risks.

Real role-playing is creative and fun. When you play a new role, you discover what really fits your personality—and what doesn't. You try on new values, behaviors, and beliefs, and discover new ways to act. All of this helps you grow and mature!

Real role-playing is part of school life. Every time you move to a new grade level, you step into an entirely new role. You are a year older—and so is everyone around you! Everything that happened in the previous grade has changed you. You have become a different person. Even if a lot of your old friends are in that class, everyone else is different, too. Exploring your new grade level lets you play a new role for real.

Real role-playing is a choice you can make anytime. Start by figuring out what you'd like to do. Let's say you want to talk to your parents about giving you more freedom. Imagine all the details surrounding that situation: where that conversation might take place and who will be involved. Get your friends to play your mom or your dad and then act it out! Run through it several times. Have your friends ask you different questions every time so you can figure out how to respond. When you role-play for real, you'll grow by leaps and bounds!

RAISE YOUR EQ

Raise your EQ, your emotional (intelligence) quotient, to live smarter!

Raising your EQ tells you how your emotions affect you. Having a high EQ boosts your self-confidence and helps you stay balanced. Your EQ helps you figure out why you're doing things—and why others might act the way they do. Finally, it helps you figure out what other people are feeling.

Raise your EQ in school to bond with others. Being around all those other students means that you have to be able to get along with a lot of different types of people. With a high EQ, you'll work better on team assignments. You'll figure out how to resolve conflicts with others, and even be able to head them off before they begin. You'll communicate better, and others will look to you for leadership.

Raise your EQ by paying attention to your emotions throughout the day. Feelings are a natural part of anyone's life and can be helpful. Some of them can be distracting, though! When you pay attention to your emotions, you can stop anger, sadness, and frustration from messing things up. Turn your attention to something other than the bad emotion. Talk to a friend, work on an assignment you like, or simply take a walk at lunch. You'll reset your negative emotions and raise your EQ at the same time!

TAKE THE CONTROLS

Take the controls because only you are in charge of you!

Take the controls to take full responsibility for your happiness and your health. When you do, you'll realize in a very real way how powerful you truly are. You'll also feel more grateful for the skills and things you have. Every time you take the controls, you'll see many choices laid out in front of you. You'll be able to explore them all!

Take the controls in school by taking responsibility for your grades and your work. If you think something isn't working well, figure out a way to change it! If there isn't enough time in class for assignments, work on them over lunch. When you can't fix things by yourself, asking for help is a great way to take the controls. You can do a lot to change things—and when you take control of your education, that's really the most important thing.

Take the controls by defining yourself in a single sentence that starts, *I am . . . .* Include who you are right now, what you love, and where you want to go in the future. *I am an artist who loves how fractals can form cool images I can paint. I am a football pro who wants to raise money for kids with cancer.* Use this as your personal motto. It will encourage and inspire you now and in the future. Best of all, it will help you figure out how and when to take the controls!

REVIEW YOUR DAY

Review your day so you can make your life easier and speed your way to success.

Reviewing your day allows you to catch little things that are going wrong before they turn into huge problems. A daily review takes only a few minutes but can pay off big. If you wait to review an entire week or month, you'll forget a lot of things and won't be able to make easy adjustments.

Review your school day in the time it takes to walk or ride the bus home. Consider any steps you took to move closer to your educational goals. If you finished all the assignments in class, that's great! Working with a group usually gives you new insights, so think about assignments you did with other students. Be sure to review the time you spent at lunch and during other breaks, too.

Review your day right before you go to sleep. This doesn't have to be difficult. Do it while you brush your teeth! You can use a journal or diary to jot down anything you want to remember later. Your notes might include the date of an event you heard about, a reminder to call a friend, or something about your family. Most of the time you'll remember the good things that happened, which can trigger happy dreams!

MIRROR, MIRROR

Mirror, mirror is an easy way to remember a key social tool that helps you get along with others.

Mirror, mirror uses your body language to communicate with other people. When you mirror someone else's gestures, you make them feel comfortable and safe. The words you speak will be heard much more than if you don't mirror the other person. Mirroring can even help you develop new habits that help you make friends!

Mirror, mirror whenever you work in a group. Listen not just to what someone else says; pay attention to how they say it. If they are upset about something, you can frown just a little or knit your brows. When they are excited, smile along with them. This opens the other person up and makes them feel safe sharing. And since groups let you learn from fellow students, mirroring is a great way to get others to share everything they know!

Remember to *mirror, mirror* when you speak to adults. No matter what's going on, mirroring their gestures and expressions proves that you're listening. It works really well when you're interviewing for a job or joining a club. When you mirror someone else, they tend to think that you are on the same level. So when you're working with people in power, mirroring them helps you maintain your own power!

POSITIVE POSTURE

Positive posture is a simple and easy way to boost your confidence and empower your life!

Positive posture benefits much more than your body. When you stand and sit up straight, you feel more confident and in control. Your motivation to reach your goals increases and your stress level goes down. A quick stretch to reset your posture can also boost your energy!

Positive posture can help you make the grade! When you have good posture, your resilience increases. That means you can tackle challenging assignments more easily. You also have the stamina to complete homework and difficult lessons. Positive posture tells your brain to stay alert!

Positive posture can soothe negative emotions. Often when we're tired, depressed, or just plain having a bad day, we slouch around. The slump signals your brain that things aren't going well. Just by straightening up, you send a totally different message to your mind. In fact, it's so powerful that the results are the same as if you have just won a game. To win every day, practice positive posture!

DITCH THE FILLER

Ditch the filler cuts out useless words that make you sound unsure of yourself.

Ditch the filler eliminates words like "right" and sounds like "um." Ditching fillers makes you sound confident. It presents your thoughts and ideas in a better light, so people will listen carefully. People will take you seriously!

Ditch the filler at school by using body language and other words instead. When the teacher asks you a question, let them know you are thinking about the answer by saying, "OK" or nodding. If you need more time, simply raise one finger to indicate that you need a minute. As long as your finger is up, you are still communicating that you are taking that minute to think. And because you aren't churning through a bunch of filler words or sounds, you'll come up with the answer more quickly!

Ditch the filler by staying engaged. When you're talking to someone in person, look them in the eye. Stay engaged on the phone by looking at that person's profile picture. You can also close your eyes and imagine that they are standing in front of you. If you use a lot of fillers, ask your friends to point at you every time you use one. You'll be able to catch each filler word or sound the moment it happens and ditch it to communicate better!

HANDS ON

Hands on reminds you that the best life is lived in real time.

A *hands-on* life is filled with fun, positive activities. When you stay engaged with people and places, you go through each day with a real connection. Your experiences mean more to you, and you live a 3-D life!

Stay *hands on* with your education whenever you can. Reading about history is great but it comes alive when you visit a museum. Science labs are all about hands-on activities! The next time you have to write something for class, go back to using a pen or pencil. You might be surprised how much more creative and thoughtful your writing is with a hands-on approach!

Keep your *hands on* all the important areas of your world. Listen to music being performed live on instruments that aren't electronic. The sounds will vibrate throughout your body and will change the way you experience the flow of the music. Go on a nature walk and collect anything that looks interesting to you. When you get home, arrange the rocks, flowers, leaves, and bug wings into a collage. Take a picture and use that as your screensaver to remind you to stay hands on!

REBOOT YOUR ATTITUDE

Reboot your attitude to stay balanced and calm no matter what!

Rebooting your attitude helps you deal with everyday problems. We all get sad, mad, or just a little cranky sometimes. Knowing how to reboot your attitude allows you to be happy more often. You'll become more stable and be in control of your life.

Reboot your attitude when things don't go well at school. Bad test grades and tough assignments happen to the best students. The trick is to not let it get you down. When you reboot your school attitude, you'll swerve around that bump in the road and head straight into learning!

Reboot your attitude with a few simple steps. First, focus on the positive. If the situation is really tough and you can't find anything positive, go inside your mind. Find something positive about yourself that never changes. Maybe you're always kind to your little sister or you feed wild birds. These little acts might not seem like much compared to the problem but trust me, they're important! When you hold that good thing in your mind, you'll realize that you can face the tough situation because you're a good person. That's really all that matters!

BUILD A STORYBOARD

Build a storyboard to figure out exactly where you are and how to get to where you want to go.

Building a storyboard gives you a real way to imagine your goals and build your future. Using photos, drawings, and words, you create a collage that represents the best of you now and in the future. Hanging it in your room or locker gives you a daily reminder of your goals. And it's easy to change as *you* change!

Build a storyboard that represents your goals for school. Use words like *rising* or *flying* to trigger a boost in grades. Add pictures of racers crossing the finish line to inspire you. As the weeks go by, paste comments your teacher has made onto the collage. Hang it in your locker to refresh your motivation every day!

Build a storyboard for your future by connecting three designs. First create a collage that represents where you are today. Then make a second collage that represents where you want to be after you graduate. Include pictures of places you might live, scenes from areas you want to visit, and people. Hang these up side by side with a little space between them. In that space, set up a third storyboard that represents the steps you need to take to get from your present to your future. The three create your own special roadmap!

OBJECTS ARE CLOSER THAN THEY APPEAR

Objects are closer than they appear—and so is your success!

Objects are closer than they appear in the side mirrors of cars so the driver can see what's on the passenger's side. The mind uses visual clues to figure out how big something is in the distance but those tricks don't work in these special mirrors. The reminder is a great way to view your life. Too often people think that their goals are really far away. They get caught up in other details and don't realize that success is a lot closer than they think!

Educational success is one *object that is closer than it appears.* This is true because no student attends school alone. Every boy and girl has an army of helpers! Teachers and counselors, parents and friends, coaches and principals are all ready to help. If one person can't give you what you need, there's always someone else around who can!

Objects are always closer than they appear! No team always wins at sports—but by playing, you get real-world practice and learn new techniques from the other team. Everyone has a bad day now and then;

working through those days builds your ability to bounce back. Check in on your progress now and then. If you're closer to your goal than you thought, give yourself a little reward! One day soon, you'll march right up and grab success!

ACE YOUR APPEARANCE

Ace your appearance by presenting yourself as a capable, intelligent person.

Acing your appearance is a simple step that provides you with a lot of great rewards. It allows you to move through the world with every confidence in who you are. Other people will be more likely to respect you before they ever speak with you. Having high marks in your appearance sets you up for success in everything you do. Acing your appearance immediately tells others that you are someone to be taken seriously!

You spend a lot of time at school every week, so *ace your appearance* on campus. It's perfectly fine to demonstrate who you are with clothes that reflect your personality. It's not fine to force other kids to look at your underwear by sagging your pants or wearing shirts that slip down and show your bra. Some schools are having so much trouble with baggy and saggy clothes they are considering making their students wear uniforms. If you don't want to be trapped in a boring uniform, ace your appearance every school day!

Ace your appearance without wasting time in front of the mirror. Put together several outfits using your go-to basics. Jeans or baggy pants might be your favorite thing to wear because they're comfortable. That's perfectly all right, as long as you don't sag them! Pair your jeans one day with a clean t-shirt. The next day, wear pants with a nice shirt or a long tunic. Cargo pants or skirts are also really comfortable, and can also be paired with almost anything. Before you walk out the door, ask yourself if others will be comfortable around you. If anyone might feel uncomfortable with your appearance, change your clothes! Show others that you respect yourself enough to wear clean, presentable outfits. They will automatically offer you the respect you deserve!

Part II

Choice Knowledge for Your Balance

RESPECT OTHERS

Respect others for who they are rather than who you want them to be.

Respecting others helps you get along with people even when you don't like them. Respect is the glue that holds a community together, and your school's community is no different. Respect for others makes you a part of that group in an important way! And when you respect others, they are much more likely to respect you.

Respecting others happens a lot at school. When you do your assignments, you show your teachers respect. By following the rules, you respect the principal who set up the rules. You even respect the other students when you show up for class on time! Respect is something that grows the more you feed it. Every time you show respect, you get more back!

Respect others no matter who they are. Respect the janitors who keep the school clean by not leaving messes behind. Respect the cafeteria workers who get up early every morning to cook your meals. Respect the bus driver who is responsible for your safety and the safety of your friends. The school needs every one of these people, so every one of them deserves respect!

RESPECT YOURSELF

Respect yourself because you are worth it!

When you *respect yourself,* you think through the consequences before you do something. Even though some of the lessons are difficult, with self-respect, you know that you can succeed. Respecting yourself gives you a whole different outlook!

Students who *respect themselves* take pride in what they can do. They don't just have friends; they have good friends who truly care about them. They feel confident enough to participate in extracurricular activities like sports, debate clubs, and the yearbook. They achieve at higher levels than students who don't respect themselves!

Respect yourself by figuring out what you do well. That way you'll always remember that you have value in the world. Take responsibility for how you behave. Know what you want from school—and from every other activity you participate in! Imagine yourself tomorrow, next year, and after you graduate to discover your true goals. Take one small step every day toward those goals, and you'll always respect the progress you're making.

YOUR BEST FRIEND

Your best friend in this world is you!

When you are *your best friend,* you can draw on your inner strength. You can face even very tough challenges with confidence. Bullies aren't able to hurt you with their words or their actions. You'll have more friends, and they will be more likely to stick around when things get tough. Best of all, you're able to be the kind of friend who really cares!

Students who are their own *best friend* aren't afraid to try new things. They feel happier because they feel positive about their lives and themselves. In school, this means you'll approach lessons knowing that you can succeed. Even when you have a tough day, you'll know that tomorrow will be better because your best friend is always there for you!

Part of being *your own best friend* is asking others for help. Not even the smartest person can do everything by themselves. When you are your own best friend, you accept that some subjects or activities are going to be challenging. By asking for help from a teacher, a friend, or a fellow student, you accept yourself the way you are. Friends love you no matter what—and as your own best friend, you love yourself!

LET GO

Sometimes growing up means *letting go* of people or things that don't serve you anymore.

When you *let go* of people, things, and ideas that are holding you back, you step into a whole new world. You walk away from pain and discover happiness. You drift away from friends who aren't growing in the same way and connect with new friends. You can see how things really are, and you discover that you're OK with that!

Letting go makes your life easier. When you let go of your instant dislike for a new teacher, the student who sits next to you, or a school subject, you chill out and accept those things. You allow things to be whatever they are going to be—and in that lies power! When you just allow things to be, you become more flexible. You still might not like science or math or physical education, but it becomes much easier. You stop fighting and go with the flow!

It's weird but true—*letting go* of the things you can't control can be really difficult. So practice by letting go of small things first. When the cafeteria runs out of your favorite food, let go by finding something else you like. If your favorite backpack wears out, let go by knowing you can find another one that will work just as well. Then when you have to let go of something big—like a friend who suddenly turns mean—you'll know that you'll be fine. You have choices, and it's time to make a new one!

PLEDGE ALLEGIANCE

Pledge allegiance to your friends, your teachers, your school—and yourself!

Pledging allegiance is all about loyalty. Being loyal to the people you meet in school connects you to a community. Your loyalty will be noticed by others, which will trigger their respect for you. Others will turn to you for friendship and advice!

When you *pledge allegiance* to your friends, you refuse to participate in gossip. Loyalty to your teachers means you help them in class by following directions. Pledging allegiance to your school connects you with the principal, the cafeteria workers, and all the other employees. You become an important part of the school!

Pledge allegiance by choosing your friends wisely. Whenever you participate in group activities, treat every individual on your team like a true partner. You don't have to be best friends with everyone you meet but do be polite. Kindness is the core of loyalty. Treat others the way you want to be treated and you'll never go wrong!

SETTLE YOUR SPIRIT

Settle your spirit to find peace in a spiritual belief.

Settle your spirit to become strong and confident. When you know what values and morals are important to you, you know how to act in a tough situation. You'll quickly let go of anger and sadness. You'll be happier and you'll be more connected to your friends!

When you *settle your spirit,* the difficult parts of attending school become easier to handle. You know right away the kinds of people you want to be friends with, so you'll avoid being hurt by people who don't make good friends. You'll realize that the rules keep you safe and help you learn. And when your spirit is in a good place, you'll automatically want to help other students—and that makes you a good friend!

Settle your spirit by thinking about the things you want to believe in. You know that gossiping about a friend is wrong but what about gossiping about someone who's a bad person? When people gossip about a bad person, it makes changing more difficult for that person. When everyone expects the worst from them, they're going to feel like they lose no matter what they do. You don't have to talk to bad people, but don't talk about them, either. Settle your spirit by doing the right thing and allowing them to find their own way!

LOVE YOURSELF

Love yourself to become a powerful person!

Loving yourself helps you stay balanced. You feel calm because you're at peace with yourself. You're able to go with the flow when you have to—and you'll know exactly when to stand up and step out! Best of all, you'll build the confidence to try new things and make new friends.

No matter what grade you're in, *love yourself* every time you step inside the school. Honestly, walking the halls and attending class can be tough. You're constantly faced with new lessons, and no one gets top grades all the time. Sports and extracurricular activities can ask you to grow even more. And some of your fellow students aren't the nicest people on the planet. When you love yourself every minute you're in school, your true self shines!

Love yourself by remembering who you are and where you come from. Who you are is a combination of everything you like and love, everything you know and choose to do, and every person connected to you. Where you come from includes your family, your friends, and everything you've experienced in life. These things make you totally unique! Mistakes and successes, sorrow and joy are woven into your spirit. You are strong because of what you've done. Let that strength carry you through each day and into your future—with love.

OFFER AN APOLOGY

Offer an apology in its true form.

When you *offer an apology,* you tell others that you regret having done something wrong. An apology asks for forgiveness for pain you've caused someone else. An apology expresses your sorrow over having made a mistake and proves that you want the chance to try again. Apologies hold friends together and build trust!

In school, it might seem like *offering an apology* isn't needed for being a few minutes late to class or forgetting your homework. Those might seem like pretty small things, but actually they aren't. Being late disrupts the attention of your peers. Forgetting to turn in your homework on time might make your teacher feel like you don't respect their efforts to help you learn. Offer an apology even for these minor infractions. You will be forgiven!

Offering an apology doesn't have to be a big production. Most of the time, a quick apology is all that's needed. Everyone makes little mistakes. We stumble into someone in the hall, we spill food in the cafeteria, or we honestly forget something. Just look the other person in the eye, say, "I'm sorry," and move on. If you make a big mistake and have to offer a big apology, look the other person in the eye and say you're sorry. Tell them you know you upset them and that you'll try not to let it happen again. Listen to what they say about the event, and then repeat your apology. You'll be forgiven, and both of you can move on!

TALK IT OUT

When something is really bothering you, *talk it out* with a counselor, parent, or teacher.

Talking it out really helps. First, it makes you feel supported because someone cares enough to listen. Second, talking it out helps you lay out all your emotions. Once they're out in the open, they are much easier to handle! Finally, talking it out with an adult keeps you safe no matter what issue you're facing.

The kinds of situations students most often need to *talk out* are feeling sad or lonely, being scared or nervous about something in their lives, and problems with friends or family. Talking about eating disorders, racism and bullies, harassment and sexual assault are also very important. Students might want to talk about the death of a friend or family member, or they might be thinking about committing suicide. No matter what you're worried about, talking it out will help!

Talk it out by finding someone you trust. The school counselor's job is to talk it out and take action! Teachers will always be there for you—so if the first teacher you approach won't help, ask a different teacher. The principal is never too busy to find someone to talk with you. Your parents, a neighbor, your uncle or aunt are all people you can turn to. Keeping the problem inside won't solve anything. Talk it out and you will triumph!

A'S AREN'T EVERYTHING

Although grades are important, *A's aren't everything.*

When you remember that *A's aren't everything,* you become a balanced student! You know that curiosity, putting in effort, and making good choices are also part of learning. Those skills are just as important as an A+!

A's aren't everything but they sure seem like they are! These days, all kids hear about is grades, grades, grades. Students compare their latest scores as if they were "likes" on Facebook. Sometimes parents can seem as though they're only interested in the letters on the report card, and news reporters compare one school's grades to another. Remember that grades are just snapshots of all your efforts. Grades are milestones on the road, so enjoy the entire journey!

Remember that *A's aren't everything* when you're worried about a test. Being worried about a test can keep you from studying effectively. If you're upset because your scores aren't as high as your friends' scores, know that everyone learns at their own pace! When you make a real effort to learn, to listen in class, to follow the rules, and turn in the work, give yourself an A+!

SHARE

Share who you are and what you have to help others and yourself.

Sharing is a powerful gesture. When you share the things you own, you get to know your friends and fellow students better. It makes you feel good about yourself and grateful for what you have. And when you find yourself in need, the fact that you share so much makes others more likely to share with you!

Everything about school is based on *sharing*. When the teacher calls on you for an answer, you're sharing what you've learned with fellow students—and helping them figure out what's important. Teachers share the things they know, and counselors share their ability to care. Even the cafeteria cooks share their ability to make healthy food!

You might not realize it, but you probably already *share* a huge amount! Every time you talk to a friend, you're sharing a little of what makes you a great person. Group assignments give you the opportunity to share your knowledge. You can share even more by connecting with kids overseas through social media. Tell them all the little details about your day. What seems normal to you might be very different to them! When you share yourself with others, you receive so much more in return!

PLAY

Play keeps your body fit and your mind full of fun!

Play is a path that heads straight to Wonderland! You'll feel better about yourself as you learn new games and hobbies. The pleasure you feel helps you enjoy life. When you play hard, you'll train your muscles. And since play makes you more creative, you'll solve problems more easily!

Playing is an important part of school. You might think of recess as the only time students play. Really, though, every gym class is another opportunity to play using your body. Every time you create a game for a class assignment, you're figuring out how to play with facts. Whenever you walk into a lab or sing in the chorus, you're taking part in playful learning. Pretty much anytime you enjoy class, you're playing!

Play all the time by enjoying as much of your day as you can. Whenever you walk through a crowd, locate every color in the light spectrum in the clothes people wear. If you spot all the colors, you've created your own rainbow! In geology or during a walk, take a trip to the center of the earth by identifying all the different layers in the earth's crust. Remember new words by drawing cartoons based on their meanings. You don't need a board or a computer to play. You only need your creativity!

RESPECT YOUR BODY

Respect your body by engaging in safe, healthy habits.

Respecting your body keeps you fit and strong. When you accept your body, you don't worry about whether you are bigger or smaller or stronger or weaker than your friends. You love the body that you have! You make healthy food choices, you exercise or play physical games, and you avoid dangerous activities. Best of all, respecting your body keeps you happy!

Respecting your body can be tough, especially at school. Gangs might pressure you to join and participate in dangerous crimes. Kids who do drugs or drink might offer you the same poison they take to get high. Boys or girls might pressure you to have sex before you're ready or ask you to practice unsafe sex. When you respect your body, you put your own needs first!

Respect your body by practicing good grooming. Shower or bathe every day. Wear clean clothes, eat enough but not too much, don't start smoking, and don't get piercings or tattoos until you're much older or perhaps never. If you feel tired or sick, get enough rest or see a doctor. Love the body you live in. You'll have it the rest of your life, so take care of it now!

SAMPLE THE SCREENS

Sample the screens gets the most from the time you spend in front of different digital devices.

Sample the screens to get the best they have to offer! When you treat your smartphone or tablet, your computer, and your television as tools, your life really expands. You'll save time by easily connecting with friends; you'll digitally track school assignments; and you'll learn about people and places all around the world!

How students *sample screens* is probably covered under your school's rules. One teacher might not allow smartphones inside the classroom while another encourages students to research on the web. School computers usually lock out certain types of websites, and TVs are used only for movies or documentaries. By providing guidelines for how to sample screens, your school is giving you a great way to look at your personal devices.

Sample screens by considering how much time you really have every day to sit with your devices. After adding up school time, homework, afternoon programs, and meals, you might have only an hour or two left. Decide which screen is most important to you and use that one first. If you get caught up in what you're doing, enjoy it! Since you placed the most important screen first, you won't have to worry if you don't visit the other videos, social pages, or chat rooms that night.

PACK YOUR BAGS

Pack your bags so that you are ready to step out into your own life!

Packing your bags keeps you focused on your future. It creates a positive sense of excitement around even the most boring task. When you know that every grade, homework assignment, and book takes you closer to living on your own, you focus more so you can capture that huge reward!

Schools help students *pack their bags* a number of ways. First and foremost, school teaches you basic skills like math, reading, and social studies. Second, attending school teaches you how to study and use your mind to solve problems. When you try different pathways to a higher grade, you pack your bags with perseverance!

It's never too early to *pack your bags.* No matter what grade you're in right now, after-school activities can give you a broader view of the world. Reading and even surfing the internet can also prepare you for life! You'll meet new people and learn new skills. You'll discover how different ideas are changing the world. The entire time, you'll follow your curiosity wherever it might lead. Curiosity is one of the best skills you can pack in your bag!

FORGIVE

Forgive those who hurt you so that you don't hurt as much!

Forgive others to make yourself happy. When you offer forgiveness, you let go of the pain. Forgiveness lets the past stay in the past. It allows you to focus on what's important right now! By forgiving others, you will also find it easier to forgive yourself when you make a mistake.

Forgiveness is important whenever a group of people gets together. And since school gathers a whole lot of different people together, forgiveness is really important there! Just imagine how many times teachers have to forgive students who act out in class. They have to forgive so they can teach that student the rest of the year.

The next time your teacher has a bad day, *forgive* him and let him return to being a great teacher the next day. When your mom or dad sets a rule you think is unfair, forgive your parents for not seeing things your way. If your friend says something mean, forgive them for feeling so bad about themselves that they lashed out at you. Forgiveness will help you move on and be happy with who you are!

WRITE YOUR WAY THROUGH

Use a diary or journal to *write your way through* tough decisions and bad days.

Writing your way through different events is a great way to figure out what you need and want. A diary helps you put things into an order that makes sense. When you feel terrible and overwhelmed, writing it all down helps you let go of the worst parts. Best of all, a journal won't ever tell your secrets!

Writing your way through can help you do better at school! First, of course, you'll practice writing, which is a big skill you'll use every year. As you write down the stories of your days, you'll find that reading becomes different. You'll wonder how books end and enjoy the assignments more! If you keep a journal when you go on vacation, you might notice things about the natural world or other cultures that help you with science, biology, social studies, or history.

Most people think of diaries and journals as a way to *write their way through* bad times but they are great for good times, too! You can keep a special journal where you record all the things that make you happy. You can create other journals for summer breaks, holidays, and special events. If you put your events journal on a computer, you can add photos, emojis, and even videos to really capture how good it made you feel! You'll have that journal for years to come as a special keepsake.

PARSE THE PAST

Parse the past to learn from your experiences.

Parsing the past keeps you from repeating mistakes. You see good things about what you've experienced, and you can apply what you learn to today. When you study your successes, you realize where your strengths lie. When you look at what didn't work, you can shore up your weaknesses or get help from other people.

Parsing the past helps you in school. Think about your favorite subject and why you enjoy learning about it. Math might be logical in a way that makes perfect sense, so you might enjoy other logical subjects like foreign languages and science. If you enjoy being creative, social studies can be your window into really different places and cultures. Reading and writing stories gives you the freedom to create the people and worlds you'd like to bring to life. When you think about what makes one subject appealing, you can find things to like about other subjects.

Make the best of today by *parsing the past.* When you make a mistake, look back at the days or steps leading up to that mistake. Was there a moment or action that led you to that mistake? If you can find that one moment or action, you can avoid making the same mistake again. The same goes for your successes! Think back to the moments and days leading to your triumph. If there is a single step or a series of actions that led to your success, you can repeat them and succeed again!

LIVE IN YOUR SUNSHINE

Live in your sunshine to bask in your special light!

Live in your sunshine so you can love yourself fully and truly. You will live a bold life on your own terms! You'll stay busy reaching for the next goal. You will dance as if everyone is watching—and you'll spread the joy that only you can provide!

Live in your sunshine every hour of the day. During school, that means building the life you want by applying yourself. It also means reaching out to friends who will make you happy and with whom you can share your joy. And since adults can be your friends too, reach out to teachers and staff.

Live in your sunshine by being your own true self. First, picture the best future you can imagine. You might be a teacher or a nurse, a scientist or a soldier. Think about the steps you'll have to take to get there. Those steps require certain skills. You might need to be really physically fit or great at math. Focus on those areas now by joining extracurricular activities. Whenever you notice that another student is really good at those skills, see if you can become friends. Every little bit brightens the sunshine that is you!

EVERYTHING ENDS

Everything ends—and opens a new beginning.

Recognizing that *everything ends* prepares you for the transition to something new. It helps you enjoy every moment of the good times, and keys your attention to the details you might otherwise miss. And by knowing that an ending is also a beginning, you're able to say goodbye to old things and welcome the new!

School can teach you that *everything ends.* Even the long-lived Douglas fir, which can survive 1,200 years, will eventually die. Stones crumble into dust and the half-life of carbon-14 is 5,730 years. In about 4.5 billion years, our sun will burn out and engulf the earth. The latest discoveries tell scientists that even our universe will eventually end. But the fir tree feeds other life forms when it decays. No particle is ever lost and everything is recycled. Endings are always new beginnings!

Make *everything ends* your call to own your power. When you're having a bad day, get through it by knowing that the day will end and will immediately be followed by a new one. That new day is a new beginning. When you're talking to your friend, remember that you might not be friends forever. You both will grow over the years and sometimes you'll grow apart. Enjoy the happy moments now. And when the friendship is over, recognize that it is a new beginning for you both!

GIVING GIVES YOU MORE

Giving gives you more friends, favors, and happiness!

Giving gives you more in every area of life. When you give, people realize how kind and caring you are. They naturally want to return the favor! Giving of yourself, your time, and your love is one of the easiest ways to enrich your life. And since giving makes the world a better place, you give to yourself as much as you give to anyone else!

Giving gives you more at school. Every time you help someone else understand their assignments, you strengthen that same knowledge in your own mind. Being a buddy for a student who transfers in during the middle of the year provides you with a new friend. Giving a few minutes of your time to straighten up a classroom or lab gives you a teacher who is more relaxed. Giving at school gets you a lot!

Giving gives you more outside of school, too. Try giving something every day to get the most. Offer your parents a little help in the morning by packing everyone's lunches. Give your friends the benefit of the doubt when they do something you don't agree with. Give your younger brothers and sisters the extra attention they need to feel confident! Give praise to anyone who does a good job. You'll give yourself happiness and build strong relationships that will give back to you!

YOU ARE PRECIOUS

You are precious, you are valuable, you are cherished!

Recognize that *you are precious* to a host of people, and you will open up to the love that belongs to you. When you expect to feel the sweetness of true affection, you discover the foundation of true happiness. You will feel cherished by the people who matter the most!

You are precious to your teacher! Sometimes that might not feel like it's true. Your teacher asks a lot of you. The assignments can be difficult; you might not like the subjects being taught; and homework feels like a drag. But your teachers ask all that from you because they believe in you. They cherish every student in their classroom, including you!

You are precious to the people who love you. If you don't feel precious, think about all the little things your parents do. Every time they cook a meal even though they are tired from work, they show you how much they care. Whenever they hand over your allowance, they are respecting your ability to manage your own money. Even when they get mad at you, they are angry because they know you can do better! Feel how precious you are to others, and you'll recognize how precious you can be to yourself!

WILLPOWER

Willpower is the determination to stick with your plan and achieve success.

The amount of *willpower* you have tells you how likely you are to succeed. Young people with self-control have stronger self-esteem. They are less prone to binge eating and alcohol abuse. They also have better relationship skills, which provides them with the support they need to reach farther.

Students who score high on tests that measure *willpower* have better grades and show up in class more than those with lower scores. Young students with willpower do better in high school, and high school students with discipline are accepted to college at higher rates. Self-control is actually more important than IQ in test scores and grades!

Great news: *willpower* can be practiced! Boost your self-control with three easy steps. First, pick a goal you want to reach. Second, decide why you want to reach that goal. If you want to spend less time on social media, is it because other people's posts make you feel bad about yourself or because you want more time for other things? Knowing why you want something helps you stick with the plan. Third, pay attention! Every time you visit your social media pages, notice how much time you spend on each site. Every week, spend one less minute on each site. Set a timer to help you keep track. Soon you'll have more time to spend on other things—and you'll feel great about the willpower you've gained!

YOU ARE BEAUTIFUL

You are beautiful because you are one of a kind!

When you know that *you are beautiful,* the world is a wonderful place. You focus on the skills and abilities that you already have. Your confidence grows, which makes you even more attractive! You feel relaxed and are able to handle whatever comes your way.

You are beautiful even when school feels like a giant contest. It doesn't matter what other kids wear or how they act. Someone else's grades and accomplishments will never take away your beauty! Being beautiful isn't about competing with others in a pageant. It's about being the very best person you can be!

You are beautiful when you accept yourself and love yourself. The person you are has a lot to offer! If you doubt this, make a list of all the things you do well. Write down all the things you've accomplished this week, this month, and this year. Remember all those times you comforted a friend or made someone happy? Those are moments when your beauty really shines!

KNOW YOUR TRIBE

Know your tribe to stay connected to friends and fellow students who can support you.

Knowing your tribe helps you feel like you're part of a warm group who cares. When you hang out with your tribe, you feel less pressure to be someone you're not. You don't have to be perfect because your tribe accepts you as you are! Your tribe offers a safe space, so you can really open up and share whatever bugs you or makes you happy.

School is a great place to get to *know your tribe.* Every time you move to a different classroom, you're walking into a different tribe! Connect with the entire tribe in small ways by helping others with their work, pitching in to keep the space clean, and welcoming everyone.

Know your tribe by connecting with people you really enjoy being around. Look into groups or clubs that focus on activities you like. Realize that although you are a very special person, so is everyone else! When you allow others to shine, you let them shine for the entire tribe. And remember that not everyone can be in your tribe. You only want people who are real and those you can trust!

CHECK YOUR SIGNAL

Check your signal so that you can always reach out.

Check your signal is inspired by the need to have a wireless signal. Without that signal, your phone and computer won't be hooked up to all the important things in your life. Just like your devices, you need to be hooked up to the people in your life! Then you'll always have the support you need when you need it.

Check your signal at school by knowing how to talk to your teachers. Most of the time it's fine to ask for help during class. At other times, you might want to talk privately. You can ask your teacher to meet with you for a minute between classes in a quiet spot. If you need more than a minute, you can ask to meet before or after school. When you check your signal beforehand, you'll always have the connection you need.

Check your signal with everyone who is important in your life. If you go a long time without talking to certain friends, connect with them through social media or by e-mail once in a while. For friends you see every day, make sure your signal is strong by listening to them—and by asking questions. They'll know you really do care about them, and the signal will stay strong!

REMOVE THE GOO

Remove the goo to clean up your lifestyle!

Remove the goo to create a lifestyle that is free of distractions and stress. You'll focus on the priorities that are really important and wipe away all the dust. You'll stay focused and know exactly what you want and how to get it. You'll feel satisfied with how you're living and who you are!

Remove the goo at school by staying focused on your educational mission. Get rid of clutter in your locker and then keep it neat. Take home anything you don't need for class or your extracurricular activities and leave it there. Walk away from students who don't take learning or after-school activities as seriously as you do.

Remove the goo by considering how you really want to live. If you constantly lose things, set up a landing pad on your bookshelf. Every time you come into the room, place your books, backpack, or anything else you're carrying around on the landing pad. If you won't need a particular item the next day, move it to a drawer or the closet for long-term storage. The landing pad is cleared of goo that might otherwise just make a mess!

DO WHAT YOU HATE

Do what you hate because you might be surprised by what you find!

Doing what you hate gives you two important pieces of information. First, it reveals why you actually don't like that particular activity. When you know why you dislike something so much, you can avoid other things that have that same component. Second, you might discover that your dislike is based on something that's not real. Even if you don't end up loving something, you at least won't hate it anymore!

Sometimes, you don't have a choice about *doing what you hate* at school. You might really dislike geometry or grammar or dissecting a frog. But to get the grade, you have to force yourself to do those things. In these cases, switch your mind. Choose to do the things that you hate and the work won't seem as hard. It might still be boring or icky—and that's all right too because you'll recognize why you dislike it!

Do what you hate at least once a month. Pick something you really dislike and decide to try it anyway. If you absolutely don't want to engage in some activity, go at it from a different angle. Research it on the internet first and see whether there isn't some small part you wouldn't mind trying. Then do just that little part! If you still don't like it, you can move on. The ones that turn out to be fun open up a whole new world!

POWER AWAY PROCRASTINATION

Power away procrastination to capture the success you want—and the success you deserve!

Power away procrastination to make the most of every day. When you take care of things right away, you build positive habits that will serve you for a lifetime. Dedicate yourself to finishing what you start, and you will race along a path where every step is filled with power. You will automatically have what it takes to see your goals through to the finish line!

Power away procrastination with everything surrounding school. The minute you receive an assignment, start working on it. After arriving home, place any homework at the top of your priority list and finish it before you do anything else. When opportunities arise to earn extra credit or join an afterschool program, grab those chances to enhance your academic success! Begin preparing for college while you're still in high school. Start a savings account, pick courses that relate to your career goals, and join clubs that focus on your skills. Every step will take you closer to that diploma and the life you really want!

Powering through procrastination is as easy as saying, "Yes!" Even if you think the task at hand is less important than something else, say yes to five minutes of work on that task. Five minutes a day every day allows you to make progress in little bites! The big surprise comes when you discover that you really enjoy the task. Even if you didn't enjoy it, the satisfaction you'll feel once it's finished is a reward that will spur you to say yes to other things. Say yes to a little now, and you'll say yes to gaining control over every part of your life!

TALK TO YOURSELF

Talk to yourself to build your confidence and treat yourself well!

Talking to yourself helps you figure out who you are—and who you want to be. Self-talk is all about listening to everything you think and say about yourself. It helps you stop thinking negative thoughts and boosts the number of times you think good thoughts! When you talk to yourself, you become your own best friend.

Talk to yourself about school when you're on campus and when you're at home. Whenever you don't do as well with an assignment as you'd like, comfort yourself with loving words! Support your ability to study by telling yourself you'll do better next time. And don't worry—there will always be a next time! School gives you one chance after another. Take full advantage of them by telling yourself positive things!

Talk to yourself about anything you need to feel better about. A lot of self-talk reflects how we think about ourselves. It can also help us understand how others think about us. Very often, young people are afraid that other people don't like them. They can feel stupid around others and end up feeling bad about themselves. The first thing to tell yourself is that you can't know what someone else is thinking! Know that you are a good person. Tell yourself about all the good things you are, and you'll worry less about what others think!

SELF-HELP HELPS

Self-help helps you take control of your life!

Self-help helps you become more confident. When you help yourself, you rely less on other people who might not have your best interests in mind. Self-help helps you figure things out for yourself and makes you more independent. Self-help helps you!

Self-help helps with school assignments. When you take control of your education, you become more motivated to complete the work and do well on tests. Self-help makes you more organized, which means that the work is easier to finish. And because you'll use the same effort after you graduate, helping yourself in school sets up your future!

Self-help helps you overcome disappointments. No one gets what they want all the time. When you're willing to help yourself, you realize that you can always try again! People who rely on others to do things for them usually don't get a second chance. Everyone has their own lives to lead, so getting a second (or even a third) person to help with something is a long shot. Help yourself and you'll be able to keep trying until you succeed!

CODES FOR COPING

Codes for coping are easy steps you can take to cope with the tough stuff.

Codes for coping are your arsenal against a host of problems! Codes are simple and easy so you can use them almost anywhere. Each code helps you tackle problems in positive, powerful ways. They give you responsibility for the most important person in your life—you!

Codes for coping at school will help you move past the little things that can be so annoying. They give you the power to do something about those things. The next time something really annoys you, try not to roll your eyes or sigh. Those actions send signals to your mind that say, "I'm annoyed!" That only makes the problem worse. Instead, maintain a calm expression. Better yet, smile! Send your mind a different signal and the annoyance won't bother you half as much.

When you set up *codes for coping,* the ultimate power resides inside you. Going for a walk is a great code to address a lack of motivation because moving your body moves your thoughts. When you feel restless or worried, do a few quick stretches. This will release the tension in your muscles and help you relax. If you just need to have fun, slap on a temporary tattoo and see who notices. Doodle something on your touch screen. Paint the window in your room with shaving cream. Laughter is the best coping code of all!

MIND THE GAP

Mind the gap reminds you to be aware of little things that might trip you up.

Mind the gap is used in the London subway to warn passengers about the gap between the platform and the subway car. Lots of people now use it in life to stay aware of things that might cause trouble. It keeps you alert to the little things you might forget about during the day. It also helps you discover unexpected issues before they become a problem!

Mind the gap in school by remembering that each of your teachers has a different set of expectations for their students. The school has a set of rules that everyone has to follow, that's true. But each teacher also has the ability to make rules for their classroom. Mind the gap between each classroom so you don't accidentally step over any lines!

Mind the gap between the different places you go during the day. A café is a great place to hang out and use the free wireless. But when you're in a library, you'll have to pay attention to the time restrictions for computer use. Be gracious and you'll not only mind the gap, your politeness will make someone else have a great day!

CRUISE

Cruise at regular intervals to avoid burnout.

Cruising is the opposite of slacking off. Cruising speed belongs to people who work very hard and then back off for a little bit so they can rest. Afterward, your mind is refreshed and your body is ready to go all day. Use your cruise so you can hit your top speed when you need it!

Cruising sounds like something you'll get in trouble for at school but it's not! You just have to use your cruising times wisely. Everyone gets an assignment that's super easy once in a while. Rather than always pushing through it so you can catch up in other classes, cruise through one easy assignment. Really engage with the lesson. It's easy, so you'll give your mind a break. And because it's easy, you might find out that it's also fun!

Be sure to power down to *cruising* speed on the weekends and during school breaks. Most students either take on too much during the breaks or do nothing at all. When you cruise, you plan some free time and some work time. Since any reading or research will be done during a large block of time, you have the opportunity to engage deeply. You might discover that things are a lot more fun at cruising speed!

GROUSE IN THE HOUSE

Grouse in the house allows you to vent your frustration and anger without hurting anyone—including yourself!

Grousing in the house keeps your private emotions, thoughts, and opinions private. When you feel angry or frustrated, sometimes just hollering about it for a minute really helps. It discharges all those emotions and lets you think calmly. By grousing only in your house or another private place, you will never hurt anyone by uttering something they shouldn't hear!

When school or teachers or your grades get you down, *grouse in the house* with a friend. If your friend's behavior at school is the problem, let a counselor or teacher you trust know you just want to vent. In the process, you'll figure out how to address the problem—and whether it's really worth your attention!

Usually, you'll want to *grouse in the house* with your best friend or someone who knows a little about the issue you're facing. That's best because you won't have to spend as much time explaining things. And the less time you spend on grousing, the faster you'll be able to move past the problem! If you can't find anyone you trust, write your complaints in an electronic journal or record your frustration on your phone. Then hit delete! You'll vaporize your worries and make sure your angry words never leak out.

Part III

Choice Knowledge for Your Life

EVERYONE HAS A JOB

Everyone has a job—and yours is to attend school!

When *everyone has a job,* teachers and students can come together to learn. It's the teacher's job to challenge you. It's your job to reach further! You'll discover exciting new worlds. You'll build new habits. And you will succeed!

Everyone has a job at school. The principal makes sure everything runs smoothly. Teachers present different activities that help you learn. Even your parents have a job because they support your education! Your job is to show up, pay attention, and stretch your mind.

Everyone has a job but no one can do their job unless you do yours. The most important part of your job is to make an effort. When you try to do the work, you learn new things. Some will be boring to you but exciting to others. The things you really enjoy might put your best friend to sleep. No matter what, your job is to finish the lessons. Every time you do, you can congratulate yourself for a job well done!

GIVE YOUR BEST

Giving your best means that you always try.

Giving your best allows your mind to grow along with the rest of you. You'll learn how to make friends when you study different cultures. You'll discover cool things about your world through the sciences. English will show you how to communicate better when you text and e-mail your friends. Giving your best means you get the best!

Giving your best helps you now and in the future. Kids who do well in school have more confidence in themselves. Believing in yourself means that when things get tough, you'll know that you can handle it. As you get older and the challenges get tougher, you'll know that no matter what, you can keep going. The success you've enjoyed at school proves that you can triumph!

Give your best every day. Show up for class on time with all the books, pens, and other tools you need. Complete your assignments by the due date. Respect your classmates, your teachers, and the principal. Know that you won't get an A every time—and that's OK. When you give your best, your work will be easier and you'll be happier!

MOVE YOUR BODY

Move your body to move your mind!

Move your body to feel great, stay healthy, and stay calm. When your body feels good, you can focus more on your assignments. Since the body and the mind are connected, a healthy body supports a healthy mind. You'll tackle challenging lessons because your physical health makes you emotionally healthy!

The best time to *move your body* at school is during PE and lunch. Give your all during PE to really get the benefits of exercise. After you eat, take a few minutes to walk around outside. If the weather is bad, try stretching. Or load your backpack with books and lift it with a single hand. You don't have to work out for a whole hour at a time to get the benefits. You'll improve with a few minutes here and there—and you'll feel great when you sit down at your desk!

Moving your body in school might seem like it's impossible. Most of the day, you're sitting at a desk. When you do get up between classes, you only have enough time to get to your next class before you have to sit down again. Make the most of that time by standing next to your desk until the bell rings. In the hallway, walk briskly. Do some stretching in front of your locker. Whenever you get to school early, take a walk with your best friend outside!

BECOME AN ARTIST

Become an artist to fire your academic achievement with creative energy!

Becoming an artist supercharges your mind. You'll discover new ways to tackle challenges. Problems become easier to solve. And because there is no "right" way to create art, you'll have the freedom to follow any path you choose!

Education goes hand in hand with *becoming an artist.* Studies have found that when students are artists, they learn faster. Their test scores go up and they can solve complex problems. Whether you play an instrument, make things with your hands, paint, draw, dance, or sing, you are sharpening your mind!

You'll find many ways to *become an artist* at school. Every assignment is a new chance to be creative! Charts and graphs can be prepared with fun colors or different shapes. Written reports become stronger when you tell true stories as part of the assignment. Presenting your research to the class becomes more fun when you perform parts of it or wear a costume. Become an artistic student and you'll excel!

VOLUNTEER

Volunteering helps you grow as a person as you help other people.

When you *volunteer,* you give the best you have to others. In return, you feel good about using the skills and abilities you already have. You get the chance to learn new ways to do things, which might help you in school or other areas of your life. You meet new people who might become friends. Best of all, volunteering makes you feel great!

Volunteering is so important for students that some states offer scholarships in exchange for volunteer activities. In Florida, one county's students can receive a scholarship for doing things like helping out with food drives, reading to children, picking up trash in a park, and other simple jobs that help their community.

Volunteering in school is usually pretty easy. Any after-school club needs volunteers to maintain equipment or set up weekly activities. Fundraising is a great way to participate in a specific group and in the success of your school. No matter where you volunteer, the growth you'll experience will make you a better student and a better person!

TUCK SOMETHING AWAY

Tucking something away saves a little money here and there to build a big savings account.

Tucking something away makes sure that you can take care of yourself. When you save a little bit from every chunk of money you earn, you discover that little additions over time add up to a lot. Even when you don't have a specific goal in mind, saving a little here and there means that you'll have money when you decide on that special goal!

Tuck something away because your parents might not always have the money for music lessons or science camp. It can be very difficult for your parents to tell you no. When you have something tucked away, they might be able to afford part of what you need—and you can provide the rest! That turns a painful no into a yes for your whole family.

Tuck something away by picking a number you can live with. Ten percent is a very easy amount to put away because it's a small part of the whole. If your allowance is ten dollars, put one dollar away every week. When you receive money for your birthday, holidays, or for good grades, consider putting away more than 10 percent. If you receive $50, it's a lot easier to put away 20 percent or even 25 percent of that. You'll have plenty to spend right away and make your savings grow faster, too!

PLAN FOR COLLEGE

Plan for college to create a big, bright, beautiful future!

Planning for college puts you on the road to your own best future. Even a year or two at college prepares you for the challenges of finding a job. You'll learn new things, and you'll be able to focus on the subjects you like. Best of all, you'll learn how to think flexibly. Nothing prepares you for a great life like knowing how to think!

Planning for college is an important part of your school years. Even students who are in grade school can set their sights on college by doing well in school and exploring extracurricular activities. When you realize that today's efforts will help a lot in college, your attitude toward school changes. You realize it's a great place to be because it leads to the life you want!

Plan for college by taking some easy steps. You already have a pretty good idea of the kinds of subjects you like and your strengths. Think about the careers you can do with your skills in math or science, or how you can apply your great storytelling abilities to marketing or politics. Join extracurricular activities that allow you to explore those skills in a new way. See whether your school offers college credit for certain classes, and look for scholarships in your junior and senior years. When you plan early, you make the road easier to travel!

TEST THE TREND

Test the trend to make sure it's right for you.

Testing the trend gives you the space to think things through before jumping in. When you test a trend, you look at it from all sides. You get to know why so many people are doing it. Then you are able to decide whether it's a trend you really want to follow.

Testing the trend is a smart move. Lots of things that might seem harmless can have hidden dangers. A number of chemicals kids use to get high are sold legally but that doesn't make the chemicals safe. A fashion trend for saggy pants or tight crop tops can cost you the respect of your friends or keep you from getting that summer job.

Test the trend by remembering who you are. No one who is really your friend expects you to follow along with something that isn't right for you. If you've thought it through and want to try a trend, go ahead! You can always leave the trend behind if you decide it isn't right after all. And remember that trends come and go. If you decide to leave a trend before everyone else, that's totally up to you!

SHINE

Shine with your inner light to fulfill your true potential!

When you *shine,* you place the best you have to offer on display. You grow as a person because you are following your true path in life.

You become happier and can handle disappointments much more easily. And you become a fantastic role model!

Shining at school might sound like you should focus only on lessons and test scores. Nothing is farther from the truth! When you shine at school, you open yourself to all the wonderful people there. You realize that teachers have lives outside of school, and that sometimes those lives are hard. Shining makes it easier to know when someone's frustration or anger isn't really about you. It helps you stay balanced no matter what!

Shine to transform your world. If something about your school isn't working, say something! Gently point out how the issue affects you and kids like you. Offer at least one way to correct the problem. And be sure to let people know how fixing the problem will change the school. Once they are able to imagine that new way of being or thinking, they will be much more likely to pitch in with the change. Shine within to create a school that shines!

RALLY FOR RIGHT

Rally for right even if the odds are against you.

Rallying for right allows you to discover the depths of your inner strength. When you step up for a cause you know is worthwhile, you trust yourself to handle any complications. You know that you don't have to explain yourself or your beliefs because what's right is obvious!

Schools have *rallied for right* ever since they started! A hundred years ago, it was right to provide every child with the same education. Schools still work hard to make students from every racial and cultural background feel welcome. They ensure the safety of gay, lesbian, and transgendered kids, prevent bullying, and even host food drives for people in need.

Rally for right by getting involved with issues. While racism and bullying are obvious places where you can make a difference, you might also work on things outside of school. Kids who don't have enough to eat have a tough time learning, so consider starting a food drive during the middle of the year. If someone in your school suffers from a disease, start an information campaign. A fire can leave a family devastated, so collect money they can use to rebuild their lives. Rally for what you know is right!

ORDERLY OOMPH

Orderly oomph adds a special kick to everything you do because you are organized.

Orderly oomph helps you stay relaxed! When you keep your locker and backpack neat, you won't lose your belongings or your assignments. You're prepared for all the usual parts of your day as well as the parts that are a surprise! You're able to focus on learning instead of worrying about the notebook that disappeared—again.

Orderly oomph is really important in school. Some schools have so many people in a single classroom that students aren't allowed to take their backpacks into the classroom. Staying organized means the classroom is safer because there aren't extra books or backpacks to trip over.

Bring *orderly oomph* into your days by keeping only what you need for each class in your backpack. Visit your locker between classes to store away things you don't need for the next class. Use free cloud storage so you can access your assignments anytime. If you use a lunch pass, hook it onto your backpack with a lanyard so you'll never misplace it. Being orderly lets you focus on what really counts!

TALLY TECHNOLOGY

Tally technology to keep from being consumed by the virtual world.

Tallying technology puts devices in their proper place. When you tally technology, you utilize devices as tools. They become one of many things that help you learn and live a better life. You can reach out to the global world and still have time to engage with the one right in front of you!

A school's rules usually *tally technology* for you. Smartphones, tablets, and laptops are usually allowed only at certain times or for certain tasks. This ensures that you learn using all your senses. It's great to see a video online but you can't smell or feel anything on film. When technology is tallied as a part of the lesson plan, virtual experiences are combined with real-world tasks. The combination helps you learn faster than either one by itself!

Tally technology in and out of the classroom. The virtual world can't be your whole world! Make time to engage with friends and family face to face. When you interact with people in real time, the stories you share flow better. People feel things more strongly, which builds stronger personal bonds. Connect off screen to connect deeply!

TEXT ALONE

Text alone means that you always text without trying to do other things at the same time!

Text alone keeps you safe. Just look at any video tagged "texting while driving" or "texting while walking" for proof! When you text without doing anything else, your messages will say what you mean. When you focus fully on one thing, you'll finish that task more quickly than if you tried to multitask.

The science behind *texting alone* is supported by much of what you do in school. Each subject is given a block of time during the day. When you focus only on that subject, your ability to understand goes up. That's because once you get into the flow of a certain task, staying with that task allows you to work faster!

To really make your life easy, apply *text alone* to different tasks you perform every day. Don't eat lunch while you're reading. Instead, allow your body to absorb the nutrients first and then allow your mind to absorb the book after the food is gone. It's fine to chat with a friend while you run laps around the track but if you need to talk about something important, stand still. You'll focus more on their words and be able to help. When you focus, you supercharge your results!

CYBER CARE

Show a little *cyber care* when you're online to make sure your posts really mean what they say!

Cyber care keeps your posts from being taken the wrong way. By clearly showing how much you care, your digital chats won't upset your friends or make people angry. The people who know you are friendly and fun in person will see that same face online. The people who don't know you will realize how nice you are!

Cyber care is especially important in school. Too many students are bullied and harassed every day. Schools are places where all kinds of kids get an education. Students of different ages, people with different skin colors, teenagers with disabilities, and really brainy boys and girls bump into each other in the halls. A little cyber care when posting about school makes everyone feel welcome.

No one deserves to be picked on, and you can set a great example with *cyber care.* Always think about your post before you hit send. If there's the smallest chance your words might be taken the wrong way, hit delete! If you feel angry or frustrated and want to take it out on someone online, go do something else for a while. When you get back to your computer, you'll see that it doesn't really matter. When others share pictures or posts, you can make them feel good with likes or tags. And if you don't have anything nice to post, don't post!

PRIVATE IS PRIVATE

Private is private means that you keep your personal business to yourself!

Private is private shelters you from gossip. When others don't know your personal details, they can't hurt you! When you respect the private parts of other people's lives, you prove you are trustworthy.

It's important to keep *private things private* at school. You might feel comfortable with your friends and even the students in your class. But hundreds more kids you don't know walk the halls! Some of them are bullies. Others might want to take something from you, and some of them are just plain mean. When you keep your business to yourself, you keep yourself safe among all those strangers!

Keep *private things private* by remembering who you're talking to. Even when you are with friends, if others can overhear what you're saying, consider waiting until you have more privacy. When you're making new friends, share only what would be OK to read about yourself on social media. Until you know you can trust someone with your personal business, keep private things private!

FLEX YOUR MIND

Flex your mind to launch your best!

Flexing your mind gives you a new way to look at things. When you exercise your brain, the lessons your teachers assign become easier. You'll also discover the wonders of the world, which will spur your curiosity. The more you explore, the larger your world grows!

School gives you a lot of opportunities to *flex your mind.* You can join the choir or the band to engage your brain with music. Learning a new language teaches you about the people who use that language and their culture. Even sports can flex your mind! Not only will you learn the rules of new games, the physical activity helps you stay mentally alert.

Flex your mind in fun ways. Learn a new dance by using online videos. Play video games where you have to navigate through a difficult landscape. Watch documentaries and historical movies to learn about the way things were. And make time to daydream! Imagining your future can help you discover ways to take steps today. Flex your mind and you'll live large!

KINDLE KINDNESS

Kindle kindness by doing the little things that mean so much.

Kindling kindness builds stronger relationships with your friends, your family, and even people you don't know well. Since one act of kindness often triggers others to be kind, it ripples out to fill your entire world! Best of all, offering kindness to others makes you happy with yourself.

Schools that *kindle kindness* are great places! All the kids enjoy being around their peers more because they feel like they belong. Students are able to focus better, and the amount of bullying goes down. These effects spin out to affect the families. Of course, teachers also enjoy working in a kind school.

Kindle kindness by doing little things to spread good feelings. If someone you know is down, pick a few wildflowers to leave on their desk. Send them a funny picture or a link to a video that will make them laugh! Put together a "year you were born" album. Help your brothers and sisters with their chores. Volunteer at an animal shelter, and always recycle your bottles and cans. It's easy to kindle kindness for your friends, your family, and the environment!

MODEL MODESTY

When you *model modesty,* you become strong yet humble.

Model modesty to truly shine. When you are humble and confident, people find you more likeable. More importantly, they also find you to be trustworthy. You know yourself well enough that you don't have to pump up your ego—and that makes it easier to get along with all kinds of people.

Schools are a great place to *model modesty.* Everyone has been in a class where one student constantly wants to show off. Often other kids end up not liking that student—which is weird because the showoff is trying really hard to be accepted! Model modesty by sharing the limelight with others. Let them answer questions and take the lead. You'll prove yourself to be humble and confident!

Model modesty by striking a balance. When you talk about things you do well, be honest—but don't brag. Don't overload people with information they don't really need to know about you. Be comfortable with the person you are, and let your actions speak louder than words!

SAFETY FIRST

Safety first uses common sense to keep you healthy and happy.

Placing *safety first* allows you to have more fun! When you recognize the dangers in an activity or an area, you can easily avoid them. That frees you to enjoy yourself, to be creative, and to really engage fully with the game or activity.

Schools are built around placing *safety first.* No one is allowed on the property until they've checked into the administrative office. The speed limits on the roads around the schools are low to prevent accidents. Everything from fire drills to how you board the bus has been adapted for your safety. With all those dangers eliminated, you can do what you came to school to do: learn!

Place your *safety first* by hanging out with people you trust. Kids who are much older than you might want something from you, so be careful. If you're not sure about how safe a situation is, ask an adult for help! Always go out with at least one friend; don't have people over when your parents are gone; and let people know where you're going. When you put safety first, you'll stay safe—and you'll automatically keep your friends safe, too!

TRADE YOUR SKILLS

Trade your skills for the things you need.

When you *trade your skills,* you get closer to achieving your goals. If you trade your skills for a paycheck, you can save money for college or buy the things you need and want. When you trade your skills for something other than money, you still get the things you need and want! The entire time, you'll be learning how to support yourself.

People *trade their skills* all the time at school. The teachers and staff trade their skills for a regular income. Parents who volunteer trade their time for the opportunity to participate in special activities. Businesses that donate to the school trade their goods for the chance to support the community. Even students trade their skills when they run for student government, work on the newspaper, or play on a sports team!

Trade your skills by finding a part-time job. You could apply at a local business to work in a store where they will train you. You can also become a certified babysitter or mow lawns on the weekends. Volunteering might not seem like a good trade because you don't earn money doing that, but volunteers learn skills that can lead to paying jobs! No matter what you can offer, chances are that you can trade your skills for something you value.

FAMILY FIRST

Family first focuses on the people who really count.

Putting your *family first* helps you remember what really matters in life. In the busy rush of your day, you might forget that your parents and siblings need you. When you put them first, you discover that they are always there for you, too!

Family first might not seem like something you can follow at school but your school family is an important part of your life. The friends you make there can support you as much as a brother or sister. Sometimes they support you more! The adults at school can also offer a lot of help, and not just with lessons. When you can't talk to your parents about something, the teachers you trust are there to help.

Place your *family first* by making time to spend at home. Your younger brother might be a pain and your older sister might not seem too interested in you but give it a try! Pick something you think both of you will enjoy. Play your brother's favorite video game with him. Ask your sister for advice on something she's good at. And every once in a while, invite your parents to watch a movie with you. You probably do all these things together anyway but when you suggest the activities, your family knows you put them first!

SMILE

Smile to make other people feel good and to make yourself feel great!

Smiling is one of those easy things you can do to make other people feel good. Smiling also makes you happy—even if you're feeling sad! It tricks your brain into thinking everything is fine, and that takes away your stress. People who smile are considered friendly and attractive. Smiling can even help you land a job or join a group!

OK, school might be the last place you feel like *smiling*. But remember that smiling can trick your mind into thinking everything's just fine. That's because the brain and the body talk to each other all the time. Every muscle movement sends signals to the brain. When your facial muscles form a smile, the brain thinks there's something to be happy about! Smiling at school can make your day go faster. It might even make your work seem easier!

Smile whenever you meet someone's eyes. You might not know that person, but you'll make them feel great! When you see your friends, you naturally smile right away. Next time, give them a really big grin and see how they react. The same goes for your family—including your pesky brothers and sisters. A little smile can go a long way toward making your relationships better.

CHOOSE A CAUSE

Choose a cause you're willing to fight for.

When you *choose a cause,* you look outside your personal space at the larger world beyond your school and your home. You notice the way other people live—and realize how good your own life is! You learn to be grateful even when things don't go well. And you'll feel good about helping others who are in need.

You might be able to *choose a cause* at your school. A lot of schools struggle with budget cuts and a lack of resources. If you want to participate in an activity your school can't afford, see whether there's a way to help make it happen. Hold a fundraiser for an after-school arts class. Ask a local printer to donate their services to the school newspaper or yearbook. You could even organize a clothing drive to support local families!

Choose a cause by thinking about things that bother you. Write an article for a civil rights e-zine. Drop a bag of food or some old blankets at your local animal shelter. Man an information booth for your local park at the summer fair. Volunteer at a museum or library on the weekends. No matter what cause you choose, you'll find a way to help!

PRAISE YOUR PARENTS

Praise your parents because they do whatever is needed to help you succeed.

Praising your parents makes you realize how much you really have. Recognizing all the great things your mother and father do for you develops an attitude of gratitude! More than just thanking them, praising your parents gets you thinking about all the little and big things they do for you. When you praise them, you feel great about your family!

Praise the parents you've found at school. Sometimes you feel really close to a certain teacher or counselor. At other times, a staff member might go out of their way to help when you're having a tough day. These people are caring for you in a way that is like the love a mother or father offers. No matter what is happening at home, you can find a parent or two at school. So praise your school parents!

Praising your parents is like offering them a big round of applause! After they volunteer at your school, you can praise them by sharing comments your friends or teachers made about their efforts. When they help you get a driver's permit, you can praise the help they gave you learning how to drive. The easiest way is to thank them for the things they do every day.

ENGAGE WITH ELDERS

Engage with elders to expand your understanding of the world and your place in the world.

Engaging with elders gives you a very different way of looking at things. People who have lived a long time have seen a lot. That means they might know exactly how to address a problem you're having. They can share the wisdom they've stored up during their lives. When you hear them talk about the things they've done and seen, you learn new ways to reach your goals!

Engage with elders to achieve your best at school! One program that matched school students with senior citizens found that the kids developed better reading skills. A study found that students of every age explain their thoughts more clearly, work better in groups, and write better after working with elders. The stories that the older folks tell can teach you how to communicate more effectively—and that helps you in the classroom, as well!

Engage with elders by starting at home. Ask your grandparents what life was like for them when they were young. Find out how they built their careers and learned new skills. If they lived through important historic events, ask them how they felt when those things happened. Once you've learned a little from them, visit older neighbors to ask them the same questions. You can even take friends to a senior care center and spend an hour chatting with the residents! If a senior citizen is painting, crocheting, or doing something else you want to learn, ask them to teach you how. Most seniors are happy to share what they know. And since you can help them find things online, you'll both have fun learning from each other!

HUGS

Hugs are a really easy way to feel great—and to make others feel great too!

Hugs are powerful medicine! Like laughter, hugs can make sick or depressed people feel better. Loneliness and worry can be swept away by a hug. The simple act boosts self-esteem because it proves that others love and trust you enough to allow you to get close. And a good hug leaves you really relaxed!

When you're at school, remember that *hugs* don't have to be given by wrapping your arms around someone. Instead, try resting your hand for a second on a friend's forearm. You can also squeeze someone's hand. A smile is the best kind of hug because you can give it at a distance!

National *Hug* Day happens every January 21. Most people think that hugs are given face to face. But you can give a really good hug from the side using only one arm. You can also link your arm through the other person's and squeeze just their arm. No matter how you hug, give the person you're hugging all your attention! And don't hold an armload of stuff between you and the other person. No one likes to be poked by the edge of a notebook, so try the one-armed hug if you are carrying a lot of stuff. You'll still give them a warm feeling—without the pain!

FRIENDS ARE WORTH IT

Friends are worth the extra effort involved in relationships.

Friends are worth it because having like-minded people around gives you a sense of belonging. By interacting with people you respect and trust, you can find your purpose. Hanging out is fun, and it reduces your stress and flat out makes you happy!

Friends are worth it at school. One of the biggest benefits friends offer is help. They can help you get through a tough assignment by sharing their skills. Sitting with friends at lunch can help you relax and return to class with a fresh mind. Best of all, a friend can just be there when you need to hang out.

Show your *friends they are worth it* by telling them how much you care. Send a random text now and then with a happy emoji. Pay attention to what they say and try not to interrupt—especially when they're sharing something important. Always say thank you, and reach out if they seem like they're unhappy or having a bad day. Friends are worth the extra effort!

KEEP YOUR BROTHERS AND SISTERS

Keep your brothers and sisters by cherishing them for who they are.

Keeping your brothers and sisters invites the world to become as close to you as a brother or a sister. When you keep others, you do what you can to ensure their physical and emotional safety. You extend the reach of your love and caring to all people even if they aren't your friends!

Keep your brothers and sisters at school by recognizing that every student is worthy of compassion. You don't have to be in the same class, share the same interests, or even know someone's name to keep them like a brother or sister! You only have to respect their right to be in school, to feel safe on campus, and to learn in the way that fits them best.

Keep your brothers and sisters by reaching out to people who need a boost. Showing compassion can be as simple as smiling at a person who looks really sad. You can help a neighbor out when they're going through a tough time by leaving a nice card in their mailbox. You can keep your animal brothers and sisters by caring for the environment or taking up a collection for an animal rescue group. No matter how you keep your brothers and sisters, your love will grow every time you offer it to someone else!

DREAMS DO COME TRUE

Dreams do come true if we have the courage to pursue them.

Dreams do come true for the people who are willing to chase them. Dreams are by their nature hard to obtain, so you'll develop courage. You'll learn how to be independent, and you'll stay focused on what's really important to you. Whenever you meet a milestone toward that dream, you'll feel great about how far you've come!

Going to school is all about making *dreams come true!* The different skills you learn in class will help you figure out how to reach your dreams. Math will help you manage your money so you can support your quest. Reading will show you how others followed their own dreams. Science will develop your ability to really study something and figure out its different parts—which means you'll be able to figure out the different parts of your dream.

You can take charge of making your *dreams come true.* First, know that feeling a little fear about doing something big or new is natural. Second, know that failure is going to be a part of your success. Each failure marks a path that didn't lead where you want—but you learned that you need to take a different path! When you work toward your dream, you stay focused on the positive, powerful life you'll have once that dream comes true. Never stop dreaming and you'll bring your dreams to life!

USE THE MAP

Use the map provided by people who have more wisdom than you for an easy journey.

Using the map gives you the benefit of other people's wisdom. Maps are drawn up when explorers learn about places other people want to go, so they are a valuable way to save time and stay safe. When you follow the directions laid out on the map, you get choices: you can pick the fastest route, the most beautiful road, or the one that stops by all the cool attractions along the way!

Use the map provided by your teachers. They have laid out the route for the entire school year, so their maps are pretty detailed!

When you follow that path, you are led through the thickets to many places of interest. Each stop provides you with several opportunities to learn and grow. Using a teacher's map helps you hit your educational target!

Use the map provided by your parents and even your friends. People don't have to be older than you to know the best way. They just have to have been where you want to go. Your parents will have maps that you'll have to follow with few deviations. The maps your friends provide might also be as narrow if you don't know much about where you're going. Keep that in mind whenever your parents insist you follow a specific route. They know a lot more about the world than you do. There's probably a reason the path is so narrow!

DREAM BIGGER

Dream bigger to create the image of everything your life can be.

Dreaming bigger moves you out of the average set of goals and into the place where you can use all your talents. When you dream bigger, you will push yourself to learn more, to grow more, and to gain every advantage. And bigger dreams pay bigger rewards!

Dream bigger at school by going a step beyond. Whenever you have the opportunity to do something extra for class, fit it into your schedule. It doesn't matter if the teacher offers extra credit for the extra effort; you'll reap the reward by stretching beyond your old boundaries. Once you've succeeded, you'll know you are able to do more than you thought!

Dream bigger in life for yourself and for others. Be bold about where you want to go. And be specific. If you want to be a veterinarian, you can work at a zoo caring for exotic species or you can start your own business and work with pets. If your goal is to help animals live healthier lives, you might find that working for a company that makes medicines for animals is a better way. You might even end up working for an animal rescue group or one that protects the environment where endangered animals live. Dream bigger and you'll dream your way to a better life!

SWADDLE YOUR SWEETNESS

Swaddle your sweetness to protect what you love.

Swaddling your sweetness helps you focus on the things that are really important to you. When you protect something, it's a sign that you really appreciate it. Swaddling prevents those things from being broken or lost.

Swaddling your sweetness is important at school. Every day you interact with people from different backgrounds. A lot of them aren't going to share the same values and priorities as you. Some won't think that college is important or they might not like sports. Others will hate reading or won't see the point in being at school! When you swaddle the activities that bring you pleasure in a thick blanket, you protect your ability to enjoy all the things that make you happy.

Swaddle your sweetness whenever you're out in public. You have the right to enjoy a movie even if the person in the next row doesn't like what they're seeing. If they get loud and disruptive, ask one of the ushers to talk to them. The same goes for any meals you eat out and even a walk in the park. You have the right to enjoy all these things without being bothered. If someone starts acting up, move away or get help. Swaddle the sweet moments to fully enjoy every day!

DATE WHAT YOU LOVE

Date what you love to bring little and big pleasures into your days.

When you *date what you love,* you make time for the activities you really enjoy. You'll stay inspired and passionate. When you work from a place of inspired passion, everything you do becomes easier! Everyone has to work to learn skills. When you really love what you do, the effort doesn't seem as hard.

Date what you love at school by signing up for extracurricular activities associated with your passion. If you love to hear about new people and the things they are doing, the school newspaper will send you to interview all kinds of people. Sometimes you'll have to report on events, which means you'll have to research the history of those events. Along the way, you'll get to know new people and new things.

Date what you love by joining groups of people who love the same things. And remember that in order to do what you love, you often have to learn all about it first! That means researching it on the internet, reading books, and talking to people who are already doing the things you love. So set up a date with your favorite activity. Start small, just like you would with a friendship, and get to know one piece of what you love. Over time, you'll build up a huge understanding of what you love—just like a relationship!

YOU 2.0

You 2.0 represents the new person you are constantly becoming!

When you recognize *You 2.0,* you realize how quickly you can change. You become more resilient, which means that you can persist even when things get hard. And since every morning brings you the chance to become You 2.0, you can always start down the path to a new you!

You have already become *You 2.0* at school. Every year when school starts again, you enter a new grade as a new person. Every time you complete a course, the new knowledge you have changes you in some way. Extracurricular activities, study groups, and sports are all chances to upgrade. Reboot who you are to reach new heights!

Recognizing that you can become *You 2.0* expands the way you think about opportunities. Every new experience is a chance to change something about how you think or what you know. Everything in your life from movies to magazines, from friends to neighbors can add something to the mix. Every experience you have changes you. Even if the change is small, you still have become a different person!

FEELINGS ARE FLOWERS

Feelings are flowers, so tend them in your garden and the gardens of others.

Feelings are flowers that bloom with many different colors. Feelings come about when we experience something within ourselves. They are precious even when they don't feel great. All our feelings are important because they show us the meaning or impact of events in our lives. Tending the flowers in your feeling garden teaches you about yourself. Tend the flowers in other people's gardens to help them do the same!

It's important to remember that *feelings are flowers* when you go to school. Every feeling creates a sensation in the mind. Those sensations don't go away just because you're busy learning. In fact, school can cause a lot of strong emotions! Tend your garden by paying attention to the feelings you have at school. If they're positive, that's great! If they aren't so pleasant, talk to a counselor about those feelings. Soon you'll be able to grow flowers there, too!

Feelings are flowers in your private garden. They also bloom in other people's gardens. When you're with other kids, see if any of those flowers match up. When you find them, you'll know that you've met someone who can be a friend! Being careful with other people's feelings shows that you can be trusted and that you're a good person. The best part about tending other people's flowers is that your own will grow into beautiful blossoms!

Final Words

Always a Student

Always a student encourages a lifetime of learning, growing, exploring, and expanding!

When you are *always a student,* you discover exciting new people. You explore places you've never been, and you learn about historical periods that offer you a new viewpoint. By staying open to new ideas, you end up surprised—in a good way!

Always be a student at school by digging into your hidden talents. If you like music, you're probably going to be really good at math (because most types of music relate to mathematical principles). Kids who can't wait until they get home to return to their latest novel or movie might discover that they can write great essays (because essays have a beginning, a middle, and an end!). No matter what you're naturally good at, chances are it will be a fun way to lift your grades!

Every hour of your day can be spent *always being a student.* Meeting new people and hearing about the food they eat and the places they come from teach you about the world. Whenever you really get into a hobby, your ability to stay focused grows stronger. Playing sports teaches your body how to move, makes you fit, and keeps your body and mind healthy. Even if you've never realized it before, you are always a student!

About the Author

Barbara D. Culp has dedicated herself to education for forty-three years. After teaching at the elementary and middle-school levels, she became the principal of a large elementary school and was selected as Principal of the Year. Currently, she is a part-time clinical supervisor for Brenau University's School of Education, and she recently founded a tutorial service company for public, private, charter, and parochial schools. Dr. Culp graduated from Morris Brown College and Atlanta University with a master's degree and an education doctorate degree in administration and supervision. She has conducted workshops and training programs on classroom management and differentiated instruction.

CPSIA information can be obtained
at www.ICGtesting.com
Printed in the USA
BVOW06s0012020317
477549BV00001B/2/P

9 781475 8350